D1713536

THE APACHE INDIANS

BOOKS BY GORDON C. BALDWIN

America's Buried Past
The Ancient Ones
The World of Prehistory
Stone Age Peoples Today
The Riddle of the Past
The Warrior Apaches
Race Against Time
Strange Peoples and Stranger Customs
How Indians Really Lived
Calendars to the Past
Games of the American Indian
Talking Drums to Written Word
Indians of the Southwest
Schemers, Dreamers, and Medicine Men
Pyramids of the New World
Inventors and Inventions of the Ancient World

THE APACHE INDIANS

Raiders of the Southwest

Gordon C. Baldwin

Four Winds Press
New York

Library of Congress Cataloging in Publication Data

Baldwin, Gordon Cortis
The Apache Indians.
Bibliography: p.
Includes index.
SUMMARY: Presents the history and the culture of the
Apache Indians and discusses their present-day life.
1. Apache Indians—Juvenile literature. [1. Apache
Indians. 2. Indians of North America] I. Title.
E99.A6B14   970'.044'97   77–21439
ISBN 0–590–07321–4

Published by Four Winds Press
A Division of Scholastic Magazines, Inc., New York, N.Y.
Copyright © 1978 by Gordon C. Baldwin
All rights reserved
Printed in the United States of America

Library of Congress Catalog Card Number: 77–21439
Book design by Elaine Groh
2   3   4   5   82   81   80   79

To my four favorite editors,
Judy Whipple
Bill McMorris
Tom MacPherson
Dale King

Contents

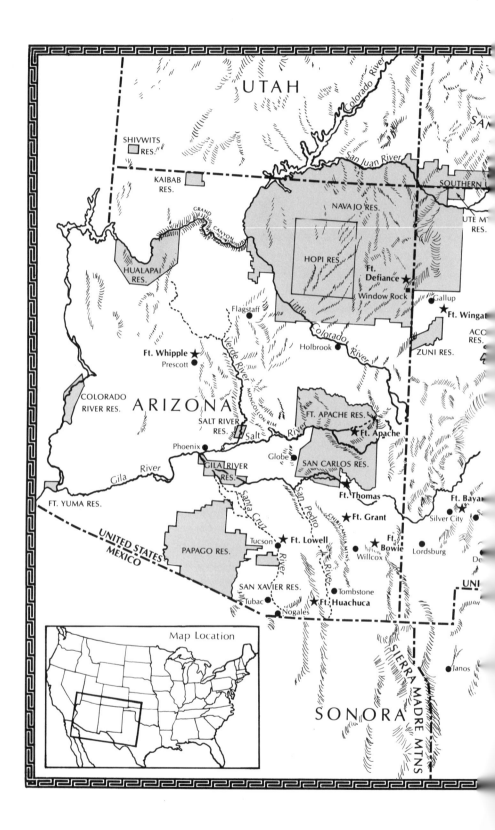

COLORADO

KANSAS

SANGRE DE CRISTO RANGE

ROCKY

KIOWA APACHES

N
MTNS

RIO Grande River

RILLA
RES.

OKLAHOMA

1 Taos

2

3 San Juan

4
5

RIO GRANDE   PUEBLO INDIANS

8   6
7
9

10

14

Santa
Fe

11
12

Pecos

13

UNA
ES.

Albuquerque

a   Isleta   ISLETA RES.

Socorro

NEW MEXICO

★ Ft. Sumner

MESCALERO
RES.   ★ Ft. Stanton

ANDREAS MTNS

GUADALUPE MTNS

Pecos River

Las Cruces

Ft. Bliss
El Paso
Juarez

Ft. Hancock

TEXAS

DAVIS MTNS

HUAHUA

SANTIAGO MTNS

RIO GRANDE PUEBLO INDIANS

1	Taos	8	San Idelfonso
2	Picuris	9	Santo Domingo
3	San Juan	10	Jemez
4	Santa Clara	11	San Felipe
5	Pojoaque	12	Santa Ana
6	Nambe	13	Sandia
7	Tesuque	14	Zia

LIPAN APACHES

APACHE COUNTRY
LEGEND

INDIAN RESERVATIONS

FORTS ★   TOWNS ●

INDIAN TOWNS ■

0 20 40 60 80 100 miles
0   40   80   120 160 km
scale

map by Gwen Hamlin

Acknowledgments

I wish to express my thanks and appreciation to the following individuals and institutions for their cooperation in providing most of the illustrations for this book:

The Smithsonian Institution, Bureau of American Ethnology; the National Park Service; the American Museum of Natural History; the Bureau of Indian Affairs; the Heard Museum of Anthropology and Primitive Art; the Nebraska State Historical Society; the New Mexico State Tourist Bureau; the Arizona State Museum; the Arizona Historical Society; Charles and Lucille Herbert and Western Ways Photos; Don Schellie and the Tucson Daily Citizen; E. T. Nichols; and Dale Stuart King for the drawings and art work of C. Randolph McKusick and Harold A. Wolfinbarger, Jr.

I am also deeply indebted to David Brugge, formerly of the Navajo Tribal Museum, for information and material on the Navajo Indians; to the late Tom Bahti for information on southwestern Indian arts and crafts; to Dr. Robert Pennington of the Bureau of Indian Affairs for material on the Mescalero and Jicarilla Apaches; to Al Schroeder of the National Park Service for material on the historical aspects of the Apache Indians; to Dale S. King for books and other material on the Apache Indians; to Eve Ball for information on the Chiricahua and Mescalero Apaches; to Dr. Donald E. Worcester of Texas Christian University for information on the Chiricahua Apaches; and to the San Carlos Tribal office for comments and corrections on the original manuscript.

Above all, however, I am particularly grateful to the late Grenville Goodwin for trying to teach an archeologist, as I was in the 1930s, to understand something of the customs and traditions of an American Indian people, the Western Apaches. Through the courtesy of the Bureau of Ethnic Research, Department of Anthropology, University of Arizona, I was able to read Goodwin's extensive notes and manuscripts on these Indians.

I also owe a great deal to my numerous Apache friends including, among many others, Turner Thompson, Nathan Antonio, and Chief Baha Alchesay.

Over the past forty-odd years I have visited every Apache Indian reservation in Arizona and New Mexico, not once but many times. I spent six summers on the Fort Apache reservation and another summer in former Gila and Chiricahua Apache country. Three extensive field trips took me through most of the Navajo reservation, including a month-long trip in the 1930s into the northern back country of this vast reservation, when getting stuck in the mud or sand was easy but getting out exceedingly difficult.

My thanks also go to Judith Whipple and Mary Lee Stevens of Four Winds Press for their patience and encouragement in seeing this manuscript through from beginning to end.

THE
APACHE
INDIANS

The Apache in Fact and Fiction

APACHE! This is a word burned deep in the pages of the history of the southwestern frontier of America, a word which immediately calls to mind ambush and treachery, raiding and warfare, bloodshed and bravery. For nearly 300 years the cry of that one word was enough to strike terror in the hearts of its listeners throughout what is now the southwestern United States and northern Mexico. Spaniards, Mexicans, Anglo-Americans, and even members of other Indian tribes all quaked at the sound of that cry.

The people primarily responsible for this 300-year reign of terror were, of course, the Apache Indians. Inferior in numbers, inferior in equipment, inferior in arms, they defeated far superior forces of Spanish, Mexican, and, finally, United States troops.

The name Apache was, and still is, almost a household word practically everywhere around the world. The Apache Indians were perhaps better publicized than any other southwestern Indian tribe. Most of the army campaigns against the Apaches made the headlines not only in Washington and New York but also in London, Paris, and Rome. The French have even applied the term to their underworld characters, their robbers and assassins.

I

Like their French namesakes the Apache Indians have been termed treacherous, cruel, thieving, immoral, cowardly, bloodthirsty, cunning, brutal, murderous. There is some truth to these adjectives, just as there would be if the same terms were applied to almost any other large group of people. There are always thieves and murderers, cowards and liars, cunning people and brutal people, in any tribe or people. That is why we have laws, police, judges, courts, and jails.

Yet the Apaches, in spite of their reputation as killers and torturers, were just as human, just as much family lovers, just as religious as most of us today. While we can't go so far as to call the Apaches angelic, neither can we picture them as inhuman savages. The truth of the matter, as we shall see, lies somewhere in between.

More gallons of black ink have been used in writing about the Apache than all the Indian, Spanish, Mexican, and American blood spilled during the several hundred years that the Apache Indians were the number one news item. Perhaps more has been written about the Apache Indians than about almost any other Indian tribe in North America. In printed word and on film it has become almost a tradition to paint the Apache Indians as the villains of the story. This is not something new. For nearly 400 years Spanish, Mexican, and American writers have been following this same practice.

An 1858 report to the Commissioner of Indian Affairs stated,

The testimony of all who have any knowledge of the Apache concur in pronouncing him the most rascally Indian on the continent. Treacherous, bloodthirsty, brutal, with an irresistible propensity to steal, he has been for years the scourge of Mexico, as the depopulated villages and abandoned fields of Chihuahua and Sonora so faithfully attest, and grave doubts are expressed whether any process short of extermination will suffice to quiet them.

Every territorial newspaper editor in the 1850s, 1860s, and 1870s had little good to write about the Apaches. Some of them even advocated the complete extermination of the Apaches. The only good Indian, so they said, was a dead Indian. One newspaper, the *Arizona Weekly Miner,* in 1869 printed a recipe for making bad Indians good: a mixture of strychnine and brown sugar rolled into pills and dropped where the Apaches could find them. Another paper, the *Weekly Arizonan*, in 1870 suggested that the government follow the practice of the Mexican officials in Sonora of offering a bounty of up to 200 dollars for every Apache scalp.

In 1864 Governor Goodwin of Arizona stated:

The Apache is a murderer by hereditary descent—a thief by prescription. He and his ancestors have subsisted on the stock they have stolen and the trains they have plundered. They have exhausted the ingenuity of fiends to invent more excruciating torture for the unfortunate prisoners they may take, so that the traveler acquainted with their warfare, surprised and unable to escape, reserves the last shot in his revolver for his own head.

The history of the Apache Indians has been written by their enemies, not by their friends. They didn't have too many friends in either Arizona or New Mexico from the sixteenth through the nineteenth centuries. With feeling against the Indians running at fever pitch, little good could be said about them.

Yet there were a few writers in the latter half of the nineteenth century who had some kind words to say about the Apache Indians. Both John G. Bourke and Thomas Cruse, two United States army officers who fought against the Apaches, said they were not cowards, that they were skillful and daring in war. Cruse even called them the greatest all-around warriors of all the American Indians.

Although much has been written about the Apache Indians, a great deal of this, both in fact and in fiction, is misinformation. Actually, most of what has been written about the Apache Indians has dealt with them as fighters or raiders or killers, telling and retelling the same old stories about the Apache wars. Little has been written about how the Apache Indians really lived, what kinds of houses they built, what kind of food they ate, what things they manufactured, what games they played, what religion they had. The answers to these and many other similar questions will be found in the following chapters.

Apaches,
Apaches, Apaches

THE Apaches are relative newcomers to the southwestern United States. We know this from several sources, one of which is a branch of anthropology called linguistics. Linguistic experts, called linguists, study the relationship between languages. By studying grammar, structure, words, and word sounds they build language trees just as we construct genealogical charts of our ancestors. Related languages are grouped into what linguists call language families. French and Spanish, for example, belong to the same language family, Indo-European, because the numerous similarities show that both were derived from Latin.

Apache languages belong to a large Indian language family called Athabascan. The Apaches' nearest linguistic relatives are located far to the north in Canada and Alaska, with a few other distant cousins scattered along the Pacific Coast from British Columbia to northern California.

These Athabascans were also relative newcomers to North America. Linguistic and other evidence seems to indicate that the Athabascans were the last major linguistic group to migrate from Asia to Alaska across the Bering Strait. This event probably took place about 1000 B.C.

4

A *Navajo woman, surrounded by her family, weaving one of the celebrated Navajo rugs on a log loom supported by one side of the hogan.*

Like all other American Indians, the Apaches and their Athabascan relatives were Asiatics. They came from a region, northern Asia, that has been the home of Mongoloid races for untold thousands of years. And most of them look more like Chinese or Mongols or Tibetans or other Asiatics than they do anybody else.

Some of these early Asiatics, perhaps forced out of their homelands by drought or famine or by pressure from more warlike groups moving up from the south and west, migrated from Siberia into the New World. This migration may have begun as early as 25,000 B.C. and lasted almost until the opening of the Christian era.

Many anthropologists believe that these Athabascan-speaking Indians carried in their baggage such new cultural items (new, that is, to the New World) as tailored fur and skin clothing, moccasins, the snowshoe, the toboggan, and the bow and arrow. The bow and arrow, incidentally, reached the Southwest long before the Apaches themselves, at about 750 A.D. or perhaps a little earlier. From there it traveled southward to Mexico at about 1000 A.D. and to South America only shortly before the Spanish arrived.

Perhaps about the beginning of the Christian era, two tribes, the Tlingit and Haida, broke off from the main Athabascan group and moved to the northwest coast, to southern Alaska and British Columbia. Within the next few hundred years other Athabascans also headed for the Pacific Coast and became the Hupa, Kato, Tolowa, and half a dozen other tribes in California. But most of these Athabascan-speaking peoples stayed in the interior of Alaska and in northern Canada, eventually spreading out and differentiating into tribes that we know today by such names as Beaver, Carrier, Dogrib, Hare, Sarsi, Slave, and Yellowknife, among others. Most of these caribou-hunting tribes live between the Rocky Mountains and Hudson Bay.

Several hundred years later, perhaps about 1000 A.D., those Athabascan-speaking peoples who were to become the ancestors of the Apaches broke off from their northern Canadian relatives and began to move slowly southward. So far archeologists haven't found any solid evidence indicating which of a number of possible routes these Athabascans may have followed in their migration from Canada to the Southwest nor the exact time that the movement occurred. Of the two most likely routes, along the eastern or western sides of the Rocky Mountains, most authorities favor the former. This country of high plains along the eastern flank of the Rocky Mountains would seem to have been an easier and more logical route than that west of the mountains.

There is perhaps even less agreement on when these Southern Athabascans first appeared in the Southwest. Some archeologists have suggested that Apaches may have reached the Southwest as early as the thirteenth century. They base their belief on archeological evidences of nomad raiders harassing the prehistoric Pueblo Indian villages of northern Arizona and New Mexico during the late 1200s. But there is again no evidence to prove that these thirteenth-century intruders were Apaches. They could just as easily have been Shoshoneans or other desert nomads already occupying large parts of Utah and Nevada.

Most historians, linguists, and archeologists have generally placed the arrival of the Southern Athabascans in the Southwest somewhere between the late 1400s and 1600 A.D. They may even have arrived about the same time that the first Spanish expeditions from Mexico entered Arizona and New Mexico in 1539–42. Coronado,

Black on white decorated bowls made by the prehistoric Pueblo Indians of northeastern Arizona.

in fact, may have reached the Rio Grande from the west in 1541 before the Southern Athabascans did from the east or north. According to Spanish documents Coronado in his famous trek from the Pueblo country of north-central New Mexico through parts of Texas, Oklahoma, and Kansas didn't encounter any Indians who could have been Southern Athabascans until he came to the plains of extreme eastern New Mexico and northwestern Texas. This would seem to bear out the theory that the Southern Athabascans migrated from Canada down the high plains east of the Rocky Mountains.

These Apache invaders might have settled down peacefully in the Southwest if this had been virgin country. But that wasn't the case. These deserts and mountains and plateaus were already occupied by other Indians, most of whom had lived there for at least several thousand years.

Scattered over the Southwest were nearly 100,000 Indians grouped in some 15 or more tribes: Hopi, Zuni, other Pueblo Indians, Pima, Papago, Maricopa, Yavapai, Havasupai, Walapai, Yuma, Cocopa, Mohave, Chemehuevi, Southern Paiute, Ute. Out on the plains to the east were more Indians, with still more to the south in what is now northern Mexico.

More than half of these southwestern Indians were concentrated among the 70-odd Hopi, Zuni, and Rio Grande Pueblo Indian villages in northern Arizona and New Mexico. The term Pueblo (Spanish for town) was given by the Spaniards to Indians living in compact stone and adobe villages who were predominantly farmers. None of the Pueblo Indian villages was large, the biggest having perhaps less than 2,000 inhabitants. Most of them probably held not much more than 400 people.

When the Spanish explorers first entered the Pueblo country in the 1540s, they found the Pueblo Indians living generally on the sites they now occupy, but there were many more villages and they extended over a wider area. One of the Hopi towns in north-central Arizona, Old Oraibi, has the distinction of being the oldest continuously inhabited town in the United States, dating back at least to 1150 A.D.

The Pueblo Indians were primarily farmers, raising corn, beans, squash, and cotton. They were the descendants of prehistoric In-

One section of the now partially abandoned Hopi Pueblo of Oraibi, founded about 1150 A.D. This is the oldest continuously inhabited village in the United States and was visited by Coronado's expedition in 1540.   TAD NICHOLS

dians who had lived and farmed in the same general area for well over 1,000 years. They lived in clusters of rectangular, flat-roofed apartmentlike houses built of stone or adobe from two to four or five terraced stories high. Each pueblo had, and still has, its sacred ceremonial chambers, called kivas. These were often circular, semisubterranean rooms like those of their prehistoric ancestors. Kivas served not only as chapels for sacred ceremonial rites but also as workshops and clubhouses for men.

The Pueblo Indians were not a tribe. There were at least four distinct linguistic groups—Hopi, Zuni, Keresan, and Tanoan, plus as many more dialects. Each linguistic group considered itself separate from the others. Each village was also independent of the others, and each had its own village chief, war chief, and council of elders.

In addition to complicated social systems, the Pueblo Indians were religious. There was an almost constant succession of rituals and ceremonies throughout the year.

In southern Arizona were a couple of other tribes of farmers, the Pima and Papago, who spoke closely related dialects of the same language. Living in one of the hottest and driest parts of the Southwest, these Indians had no need for solidly built houses. They lived in round, cone-shaped dwellings of poles and brush covered with a layer of dirt. The Pimas were able to irrigate their fields of corn, beans, squash, and cotton with water from the Gila and Salt Rivers. But the Papagos, not having any permanent rivers in their desert land to the south, had to resort to dry farming and consequently looked to wild plants and animals for much of their food supply. In fact, the Papagos ate so many mesquite beans that they were often called the Bean People. Although the Pimas had a fairly strong tribal organization, most Papago villages were politically independent.

Partially excavated pueblo of Chettro Kettle, one of the many large prehistoric ruins in Chaco Canyon National Monument, New Mexico. The circular rooms in the main structure are kivas, with a great kiva out in front.

NATIONAL PARK SERVICE

Papago Indian village in southern Arizona. TAD NICHOLS

In western and northwestern Arizona seven other southwestern Indian tribes spoke dialects of the Yuman language. The lower Colorado River Yumans—the Cocopa, Yuma, Maricopa, and Mohave, plus a number of other smaller Yuman-speaking tribes which have since either merged with the others or have become extinct—were farmers. But they did little or no irrigating, as the Colorado River was too big and too uncertain a river to work with. As a result, they were indifferent farmers, supplementing their scanty crops of corn, beans, and squash with wild plants which grew abundantly along the river banks. Unlike most other southwestern Indians, who had an absolute horror of anything living in water, these Yumans regarded fish as a welcome addition to their diet. Like the Pimas and Papagos, they built earth-covered pole and brush houses, grouping them in scattered settlements along the river.

What these lower Colorado Yuman-speaking peoples lacked in clothing, which was a great deal, they more than made up for in paint. Tattooing was universal on the faces of men and women, and both faces and bodies were also liberally coated with black, red, white, and blue paint.

Although most of these Yumans had a strong sense of tribal unity, there was little formal government. Most Yumans were warlike, fighting not so much for loot or land but for war honors, for prestige. Generally they fought with other Yuman-speaking tribes, but they also fought Pimas, Papagos, and Paiutes.

The three other Yuman-speaking tribes—the Havasupai, Walapai, and Yavapai—were primarily hunters and gatherers, only occasionally farming small patches of land around springs. The Yavapai roamed over west-central Arizona from the Colorado to the Verde River and beyond. To the north and northwest lived the Havasupai and Walapai, the Havasupai in Cataract Canyon and the Walapai in northwestern Arizona just south of the Colorado River.

Up in the plateau and desert country fringing the northern and northwestern borders of the Southwest lived three Shoshonean-speaking tribes: the Utes in southern Colorado and Utah, the Southern Paiutes in Utah and Nevada, and the Chemehuevi in eastern California.

All of these tribes, including the Havasupai, Walapai, and Yavapai, were nomadic and had few permanent houses and no large villages. They built only temporary shelters of poles and brush, sometimes covering them with skins, sometimes with brush. Their social and political organization was usually as simple as their way of life.

To the east, in the high plains country from Wyoming southward to Texas, were still other Indian tribes, the Cheyenne and Arapaho to the north, the Comanche and Kiowa to the south.

These, then, were the Indian tribes in and around the Southwest when the vanguard of the Athabascan-speaking peoples from the north, the Apaches, appeared on the scene.

The country into which they stumbled hasn't changed too much in 400-odd years. Millions of people have, of course, moved into the region. The Indians themselves have remained much as the Spaniards found them. Here and there are modern cities, and super-highways crisscross the countryside. But a lot of the land is re-

Desert country of central and southern Arizona. NATIONAL PARK SERVICE

markably as Coronado found it. The march of civilization has but lightly touched the grandeur of the Grand Canyon or the startling colors of the Painted Desert and Monument Valley. Four hundred years has not dimmed the majesty of Coronado's mountains, sometimes bleak and rocky, sometimes green and soft with pinyons and pines and high grassy meadows. Much of this is still wild country.

This is an exceedingly dry land. Rivers are few: the Colorado and Little Colorado in the north and west, the Rio Grande and Pecos in the east, and the Gila River and its tributaries sprawling across the south, while still farther south are the Sonora and Yaqui Rivers in northern Mexico.

Yet this was, and is, far from barren desert. Most of the higher plateaus and mountains are covered with trees—juniper, pinyon, and pine. Even the desert is carpeted with numerous varieties of cacti, century plants (mescal), clumps of grass, palo verde, and mesquite trees, as well as willows and cottonwoods.

In places this might seem to be a land fit only for rattlesnakes and lizards and jackrabbits. All these were here in abundance, including at least sixteen different varieties of rattlesnakes. But this desert zoo also had its share of insects, rats and mice, hawks, owls, eagles, and scavenging buzzards. There were even such big game animals as deer, bighorn sheep, and antelope.

The Spaniards called this country Apacheria, Apache land. It was enormous, ranging from the western Arizona deserts eastward across Arizona to the high plains east of the Pecos River in eastern New Mexico and western Texas, and from the high plateau country of northern Arizona and New Mexico six hundred miles southward deep into the present Mexican states of Sonora and Chihuahua.

This, then, was the country into which the migrating Athabascans suddenly found themselves in the late fifteenth or early sixteenth centuries. In contrast to most of the high plains country through which they had been slowly moving southward, the Southwest was teeming with thousands of already long-established Indian inhabitants.

At first these invading Athabascans probably didn't make much of an impact upon either the country or its peoples. It took them time to learn the lessons necessary for survival in this desert and mountain country so different from their northern Canadian homeland. It also took them time to learn about the other tribes with which they came in contact and their ways of life, often different from their own. Once they learned their lessons, however, they exploded with a blast heard around the world.

We don't know what these Southern Athabascans called themselves, if anything. It might have been something like Dineh, meaning the People, as that's the way most of them have thought of themselves in historic times. In any event, "Apache" is a name given to them by outsiders, not by themselves.

The term Apache itself first appeared as Apades or Apiches in Spanish documents relating to Juan de Onate's colonizing venture to New Mexico in 1598. The origin of the name is, however, obscured by time. The most likely explanation seems to be that the name was borrowed from Indians bordering on the Apaches, who knew the Apaches long enough and well enough to have a term for them. This was the usual method of naming tribes throughout the early Spanish period of exploration and colonization in the Southwest.

But from what other tribe was the name borrowed? Some authorities believe it was derived from the Zuni Indian word Apachu, meaning enemy, a term the Zunis use for the Navajos, as Apaches de Navajo. Others suggest that the name came from the Yuman-speaking Yavapai Indians of north-central Arizona, who call people Apatieh or Apadje. Still others say it came from the Ute Indians of southern Colorado, who call Southern Athabascans Awatche.

Wherever the word Apache came from, the Spaniards began using it in 1598 and continued to use it from that date on. Yet even after that we can't be sure that the term Apache always referred to Southern Athabascans, that is, Apaches. The Spaniards had the exceedingly bad habit (a habit that is still hanging on today, even among some anthropologists) of applying the name Apache to many other southwestern Indian tribes merely because these particular Indians happened to look or act like Apaches or because they chanced to be in the same general region where Apaches had once been found.

Nor do we know in most cases just which of the various groups of Apaches was indicated by any one report. For there were not one but seven distinct divisions of Apaches (Southern Athabascans) within historic times, based on territorial limits, culture, and language. These were the Navajo, Western Apache, Chiricahua, Mescalero, Lipan, Jicarilla, and Kiowa-Apache. You might be surprised to find the Navajos in this list, since the Navajos are almost invariably regarded as a distinct tribe, completely separate from the Apaches. Actually, 500 years ago Apaches and Navajos formed a single group physically, linguistically, and culturally. Today, however, and probably for the past several centuries as well, the two have grown farther and farther apart culturally and territorially. Thus, following modern custom, the term Apaches will normally only apply to the six Apache tribes, with the Navajo being considered a separate and distinct tribal unit.

We don't know just where or when the Southern Athabascans separated into these seven divisions. The split may have already started on the long journey southward from Canada. According to some linguists, the first divergence among the Apachean languages occurred only 400 to 500 years ago. This would be just about the time the first Southern Athabascans hit the Southwest.

Linguists have recently divided the Southern Athabascan languages into an eastern and a western group. The former consists of the Jicarilla, Lipan, and Kiowa-Apache, the latter of the Navajo, Western Apache, Chiricahua, and Mescalero. It should be emphasized that these are not distinct languages. It would be more accurate to call them dialects. All Southern Athabascan dialects are relatively similar and closely related. Navajos and Western Apaches, for example, can readily converse with each other.

The three tribes of the eastern group remained on the plains, while those of the western group split off and largely settled west of the Rio Grande in western and southern New Mexico. The areas occupied by these seven Southern Athabascan groups varied greatly throughout their history. Pressure first by the Pawnees, Utes, and Comanches in the north, followed by the French from the east, the Spanish and later the Mexicans from the south and west, and finally by the Americans, caused the various Apache groups to shift from one locale to another until they were eventually concentrated in certain geographic regions. These are the regions where we find them today.

The Navajo were originally located in northwestern New Mexico and extreme northeastern Arizona. The Western Apache occupied an area in eastern Arizona bounded roughly on the north by Flagstaff and on the south by the Santa Catalina and Rincon Mountains. The Chiricahua were located in southeastern Arizona and western and southwestern New Mexico, with an extension into northern Mexico. On the east side of the Rio Grande in southern New Mexico were the Mescalero Apaches. The Jicarilla ranged over northeastern New Mexico and southeastern Colorado. The last two Apache groups, the Lipan and Kiowa-Apache, lived out on the plains, the Kiowa-Apache in southwestern Kansas and western Oklahoma and the Lipan farther to the south in the southern Texas Panhandle.

3

The Apaches
in
History

THE Apache Indians first splashed across history's pages with Francisco Vasquez de Coronado's Spanish expedition of 1540–42. Hunting for the so-called Golden Cities of Quivira according to Mexican legends, the Spaniards had come up from Mexico into the southwestern United States. But instead of cities of gold, all that they had found were the stone and mud villages of the Pueblo Indians. These Indians had no gold, no silver, no precious stones except turquoise.

The Pueblo Indians were as disappointed as these white-faced invaders with their shiny breastplates and helmets and the huge four-footed animals which they rode. The Indians didn't like the overbearing attitude of their uninvited guests, but they couldn't do much about it. They soon found that their own bows and arrows and spears were no match for armor and guns and horses.

After spending the winter in the Pueblo villages on the Rio Grande, Coronado learned from an imaginative captive Plains Indian about a land to the northeast which was rich in gold and silver. Coronado, like most other New World adventurers of that era, was a sucker for tales of treasure. He fell for the story and set out across the eastern plains with his army.

Coronado didn't find any gold or silver. But he did run across Apache Indians, the first to be reported. These were buffalo-hunting nomadic Indians living in conical, pole-framed, hide-covered tipis on the high plains north of the Canadian River in what is now the Texas Panhandle.

As one Spanish report tells us:

At the beginning of the plains of the cattle [as the Spanish called the buffalo] we met some Indians, called Querechos by the people of the terraced houses [the Pueblo Indians]. They did not live in houses, but carried some poles with them which they put together at their camping places in order to make a sort of shack which they used as houses. They fasten these poles at the top and spread them at the base, covering the whole thing with cattle [buffalo] hides which they carry along.

This, along with other contemporary Spanish descriptions, almost certainly fits what we know of later Apachean life in Arizona and New Mexico. These Plains Indians were nomadic; they followed the bison herds, dressed in skins, used dogs as beasts of burden, and worshiped the sun. They may even have farmed a little in favorable river valleys during the summer months.

At this time, in 1541, these Querechos were on friendly terms with at least the easternmost of the Pueblo Indians. With them they carried on a thriving trade, bartering buffalo hides and buckskins and meat for corn, beans, squash, and cotton cloth.

Coronado found still more Indians farther to the east and also to the north of the Querechos. While all of them hunted buffalo, some lived in tipis, some in grass houses, some raised corn, others didn't. One group, called the Teyas (meaning People to the East) by the Pueblo Indians, may have been a division of the widespread Caddoan-speaking peoples of the southern plains, probably the Wichita, linguistic relatives of the better known Pawnee Indians in Nebraska. Some Spanish reports said that the Teyas were enemies of the Querechos (Apaches) and that they painted themselves.

After his fruitless search on the high plains for the Golden Cities of Quivira, Coronado returned to the Rio Grande, spent

Pueblo of Zuni, New Mexico, as it looked in 1879. The mesa in the background is the sacred Corn or Thunder Mountain, which provided a refuge for many Zunis from invading Spaniards in 1540 and later.

SMITHSONIAN INSTITUTION, BUREAU OF AMERICAN ETHNOLOGY

another miserable winter with the Pueblo Indians, and then set out for Mexico City. He had found no cities of gold, no fabulous treasure, and he was glad to see the last of the Southwest. Two Franciscan friars elected to remain behind, and, as might be expected, both were martyred within a short time. The small band of sheep that had been left with the friar at Pecos probably didn't last much longer.

As a result of written reports by various members of Coronado's party, we know there could not have been any Southern Athabascans closer to the Pueblos than extreme eastern New Mexico. These records show that the Pueblo territory between the Hopi villages in northern Arizona and the easternmost of the Rio Grande pueblos, Pecos, was completely unoccupied by any other people. Nor were there any Apaches in eastern and southeastern Arizona in the country later to become the home of the Western Apaches and Chiricahuas. This region, from the San Pedro River to Zuni Pueblo, was apparently uninhabited at this time. It was so reported by Coronado and others of his expedition who had made nearly a dozen trips across this particular land and found no signs of Indians. There was, however, a regular trade route across this deserted country from the Pimas and their Sobaipuri cousins up to Zuni Pueblo. From this it seems likely that the Querechos (Apaches) represented only the advance guard of the southward-migrating Southern Athabascans. The main body hadn't yet arrived.

For the next forty years we know very little about what was happening in the Southwest, as the Spaniards left the Pueblos and other southwestern Indians alone. The Spaniards hadn't forgotten about them. They had just been too busy pushing the frontier steadily northward from central Mexico as they discovered rich silver and other deposits and new cattle ranges. Hard on the heels of the miners and cattlemen came priests to establish missions and convents, along with, of course, soldiers to protect them from the heathen Indians.

By 1581 civilization had reached within 300 miles or so of what is now El Paso, Texas. Consequently, when the next expedition left Santa Barbara in Chihuahua that year for the Pueblo country, they opened up a brand new route. Instead of going up the west side of the rugged Sierra Madre Mountains through Sonora and eastern Arizona, as Coronado had done, Captain Francisco Chamuscado, a veteran frontier officer, and his small party kept to the eastern side of the mountains, traveling down the Conchos River to the Rio Grande and up that river directly into the heart of the Pueblo country. They found no wandering Indians in the Pueblo area, but they did find Indians they called Vaqueros living in the same general area and with the same customs as the Querechos of Coronado's time.

Taos Pueblo in northern New Mexico in 1879. This was one of the many pueblos visited by Coronado's Spanish army in 1540.

SMITHSONIAN INSTITUTION, BUREAU OF AMERICAN ETHNOLOGY

There is little doubt that these Querechos and Vaqueros were one and the same people, just as there is little doubt that they were also Apaches. During the intervening forty years they had moved westward a little closer to the Pueblos, from the Texas Panhandle to eastern New Mexico.

In 1582 another Spanish expedition led by Antonio de Espejo toured most of the Pueblo country, including the Verde Valley in Arizona, where they found Indians Espejo called Querechos. These Querechos, however, were not Apaches. They were Yuman-speaking Yavapai Indians. There were no Southern Athabascans anywhere in Arizona at that time.

Hopi Pueblo of Mishongnovi, with Shipaulovi Pueblo perched on a distant section of the mesa to the right, as they looked in the 1870s.

SMITHSONIAN INSTITUTION, BUREAU OF AMERICAN ETHNOLOGY

Other Spanish explorers over the years called Indians living around El Paso and to the south Querechos, or they gave them other names—Janos, Jocomes, Mansos, Sumas, Jumanos (Painted People)—and some writers still believe they were Apaches. These people were not Apaches either. So far as we know, no Apaches crossed into what is now Mexico until the late seventeenth century.

In 1598 the Spaniards came back to the Pueblo country, this time to stay for good. Don Juan de Onate, the new governor, brought with him hundreds of soldiers, colonists, and Franciscan priests, along with 83 wagons and over 7,000 head of cattle, horses, and sheep. Marching up the Rio Grande from Chihuahua, Onate founded the colony of New Mexico in the heart of the Pueblo country.

The trail blazed by these wagons and carts from what is now Durango in northern Mexico to the Pueblos of the upper Rio Grande became the "camino real," or public highway, linking this far-flung New Mexico outpost with civilization in the south. This was the most important wagon road in the Southwest for the next two centuries.

Not very long after Onate arrived in New Mexico, he used the term Apache for the first time. We aren't sure from whom he got the name. The most likely bet is that he got it from the Utes, some of whom could have been along the upper Rio Grande. For the next several years the buffalo-hunting Indians on the plains of eastern New Mexico were reported sometimes as Vaqueros, sometimes as Vaquero Apaches, sometimes as plain Apaches. Within a few more years, however, the word Apache was in common use for these Indians.

When the Spaniards first ran across the Apaches in 1541 on the plains, the Apaches were a peaceful, nomadic people. At least they were peaceful toward the Spaniards, whom they had just met. But they must not have been toward the Teyas (Wichitas), as the latter termed themselves enemies of the Apaches. Indians had been fighting other Indians off and on for hundreds of years. The Teyas, for example, or possibly some other Plains Indians, had raided and destroyed a number of Pueblo Indian villages east of the Rio Grande as early as 1525, fifteen years before the Spaniards came. Coronado's reports also said that although the residents of Pecos, the easternmost of the Rio Grande villages, traded with the Plains Indians, they would not let the visiting traders remain in the Pueblo overnight because they did not trust them.

Most Indians probably engaged periodically in intertribal warfare long before 1540. While the Pueblo Indians were less warlike than their neighbors, they could not have survived if they hadn't fought at times. Each pueblo had its own war priest and warrior organization which waged war against nomadic raiders and other pueblos. Fear of witchcraft seems to have been a cause of some fights between pueblos.

In the Great Pueblo Period, from around 1100 to 1300 A.D., most pueblos were compact, multiunit forts, presenting high blank walls to the outside world, walls that could be scaled only by ladders. Many villages were built on purely defensive sites—on top of steep mesas or the flat summits of rocky hills and inside natural caves or rock shelters with sheer-walled approaches. Archeologists have often blamed warlike nomads from the north for this. This may have been true in some cases, but it seems more likely that the majority of the conflicts were among the Pueblo Indians themselves.

Keet Seel cliff dwelling in Navajo National Monument, northern Arizona.

Archeologists have even dug up numbers of prehistoric Pueblo Indian skeletons with arrowheads embedded in their bones or with skulls battered in by what could only have been heavy war clubs.

The Yuman-speaking tribes on the lower Colorado River were more warlike than most other southwestern tribes. They fought largely with their Yuman-speaking neighbors, where fighting was a national sport to gain honor and prestige. But it was still quite bloody warfare at times. Most Plains Indian clashes also probably had the gaining of war honors as their chief motive. Conflict sometimes arose over disputes about hunting grounds and in retaliation for acts of violence or blood revenge.

The Spaniards didn't start warfare between Indian tribes in the Southwest. But these newcomers unwittingly gave the Apaches and other Indians the means and the opportunity for a greatly expanded warfare. This was something the Spaniards did not want but could not stop.

It was not the Spaniards' light skin color that most impressed the Pueblos and Apaches and other southwestern Indians: it was their horses and their guns. At first this peculiar combination of horse and man was looked on as a monster that could magically split itself into two distinct parts. It took a while for Indians to understand horses as something apart from these new enemies, something that might be useful to them.

The Indians eventually learned that they, like the Spaniards, could also ride and that horse meat was good to eat. When the Apaches started raiding, they ate the first horses they captured, along with cattle, mules, and other animals. Here was a food supply much handier than buffalo or deer. Besides, the Spanish horses and cows could be driven right to their camps, whereas buffalo or deer had to be killed where they found them, and the meat then had to be packed to camp.

Most Plains Indians seldom ate horses, preferring, instead, to

Plains Indian horse travois.

SMITHSONIAN INSTITUTION, BUREAU OF AMERICAN ETHNOLOGY

use them for riding and for pack animals to replace the dog travois. Their experience with dogs as pack animals prepared them to look on the horse as a bigger, stronger, and more useful dog, which relieved them of carrying heavy loads and aided them in hunting buffalo. In fact, most Plains Indians ate dogs more often than they did horses.

The Apaches, however, developed an especial appetite for horses, mules, and burros. Particularly in later days when most Apaches were living in mountain retreats, they regarded horses as food rather than as riding animals. If they needed horses to hunt or raid, they stole them, rode them until the animals were ready to drop dead, and then ate them. That was why most Apaches never became the horsemen that their neighbors, the Plains Indians, became. In fact, many Apaches preferred to fight on foot. The Lipan Apaches and probably the Kiowa-Apaches were exceptions. Being true Plains Indians, they were expert horsemen and valued their horses highly, a warrior's favorite war horse invariably being staked beside his tipi at night.

Although the sedentary Pueblo Indians early learned to use horses, they rarely rode or used them to farm. Their small plots were farmed by hand with hoe and digging stick. They valued horses primarily for bartering with Plains Indians for jerked dried buffalo meat and buffalo robes. Goats probably fed more New Mexico Pueblo Indians than did any other animal, while sheep eventually made the semisedentary Navajo Indians self-sustaining.

Popular beliefs that the Indian mustang sprang from horses lost by the Coronado and DeSoto expeditions in 1540–42 are nothing but myths. Coronado brought some 1,500 horses, mules, and other animals into the Southwest, while DeSoto, sailing from Cuba to Florida and thence crossing to the Mississippi, had about 250 horses and a few mules. But practically all of these animals can be accounted for, either through natural death by starvation or sickness or through killing by Indians. The latter hadn't yet learned that horses represented a commodity that they might use. Incidentally, only 2 of Coronado's horses were mares, and both of these were satisfactorily accounted for.

There was only one place where the Indians around the borders of the Southwest could have gotten their first horses. That was the Spanish settlements founded by Onate in 1598 along the upper Rio Grande in New Mexico. Onate brought in vast herds of horses and mules, along with oxen, goats, and sheep. From then on the horse population of the Spanish villages went up and down, while among Indians it went steadily upward. There are records of replacement horses and mules and other livestock coming up from Mexico by the thousands all throughout the seventeenth and eighteenth centuries.

The Apaches were probably the first Indians in what is now the United States to acquire horses. Not until 1606 do we find definite reports of Apache raids. In that year and again in the following year Spanish forces were sent out against "marauding Apaches." In 1608 another Spanish document states, "The Spaniards and Christian and peaceful natives in New Mexico are frequently harassed by attacks of the Apache Indians who destroy and burn their pueblos, waylay and kill their people by treachery, steal their horses and cause other damage."

The Apaches had stopped being friends with the Spaniards and with the Pueblo Indians. Thus began a conflict that was to last for nearly 300 years.

The Apaches may have eaten the first horses they stole, as there is no mention of mounted Apaches until some time between the 1630s and 1650s. Indian attempts to ride the first horses must not have been easy.

Other neighboring Indians began picking up horses within a short time, perhaps originally through trade with the Apaches. However, none of these Indians became true horse Indians before 1630 and probably not until a decade or two after that.

Horses soon became the most wanted items that the Spaniards of the New Mexico settlements had, for trade and bribe as well as for stealing. The Spanish policy from the beginning was to play tribe against tribe. There was never any real peace with the Plains tribes, only truces, during which the Spanish regularly traded off horses, along with tobacco and corn, for buffalo robes.

Many Plains buffalo-hunting Indians were already nomadic long before the Spaniards arrived. Horses made them even more nomadic, extending their range tremendously. They could now cover in a day distances that had formerly taken them a week by dog

Western Apache woman on horseback with burden bag behind saddle and grass-covered wickiup in background.

WESTERN WAYS PHOTO BY CHARLES W. HERBERT

travois. Horses turned Plains Indian warfare into even more of a game and food hunting into the liveliest form of the chase. The horse was the first form of property that could make a warrior rich in almost no time at all. Its ostentation value was enormous. Moreover, the horse allowed the Indian to double and triple the quantity of his personal and household possessions. A horse could pull a travois loaded with a tipi and at the same time carry a woman and several youngsters.

The adoption of the gun took much longer than that of the horse. The Apaches and other Indians owned a vast number of horses before they owned guns, at least guns that could be used as firearms. A gun without powder or lead didn't make nearly as good a weapon as a heavy war club or a spear. Guns could be captured or stolen fairly readily, but getting sufficient powder and lead was much more difficult. Furthermore, understanding the mechanics of these noisy and dangerous weapons and learning how to use them successfully were accomplishments that didn't come easily.

Actually, guns did not become a major factor in Apache hunting and warfare until the nineteenth century, when white traders introduced them in quantity, along with a dependable supply of powder and lead. Meanwhile, the Apaches continued to use their traditional weapons—the bow and arrow, the war club, and the spear. Together, however, the horse and the gun transformed the Stone Age Apache warrior into perhaps the most formidable and greatest all-around fighter and raider the world has ever known.

Now let's see how and where these Southern Athabascans split up into their various tribal subdivisions. In the middle and late 1500s the only Apaches mentioned were those called Querecho or Vaquero Apaches, then located east of the Pueblo country in eastern New Mexico and the western Texas Panhandle. They may have been the only Southern Athabascans in the Southwest in 1540.

If so, they weren't alone for long. Other Southern Athabascans, perhaps forced southward by droughts in the plains area in the late 1500s, came into New Mexico from the northeast, probably from the eastern Colorado plains. These were the Navajos, the first of the farming Apaches to enter the Southwest. They were mentioned by the Spaniards as being in the mountains west of the upper Rio Grande in 1598, the probable dinetah, or original homeland, of the Navajos in New Mexico. They didn't begin to spread very far to the south or west until the 1700s. They had presumably borrowed their farming and pottery from sedentary groups of Plains Indians before they arrived, and they borrowed still more from the Pueblo Indians in the 1600s and 1700s. Like all Southern Athabascans, they borrowed ideas and customs wherever and whenever they could. By 1622 these Apaches de Navajo, as the Spaniards called them, were reported as raiding Jemez

Pueblo. They continued raiding all the Spanish settlements and Indian villages throughout the Spanish period, with only brief intervals of peace. Unlike most Apaches, the Navajos didn't eat all the sheep they stole but began building up their own herds.

In the meantime, other groups of probably nonfarming Southern Athabascans had been gradually moving southward and westward from the plains to the north, perhaps also spurred on by the droughts of the late 1500s. Some time between 1580 and 1630 a lot of them crossed the Rio Grande into the mountains of western New Mexico south and west of the Pueblo country. About the same time the Spanish began to apply different names, based on geographic or cultural distinctions, to Apache groups on either side of the Rio Grande. Up to the last decade of the 1700s they referred to those Apaches west of the Rio Grande as Gila Apaches. These eventually split up into the various groups of Chiricahua and Western Apaches that were so designated after 1800. Benavides, writing in 1634, described the range of the Gila Apaches as being west of present-day Socorro in west-central New Mexico. Far to the northwest, he said, were the Navajo Apaches.

To those Southern Athabascans who remained behind on the east side of the Rio Grande the Spaniards bestowed an almost bewildering variety of names. Some Apaches living near the Rio Grande they called Perillo Apaches. Others to the south they termed Sierra Blanca (White Mountain) Apaches, from the major mountains between the Rio Grande and the Pecos River. After 1680 most of these Apaches moved north as far as the Sandia Mountains near Albuquerque and became known as the Faraon Apaches. Still later, after 1726, the name Natage Apaches replaced Faraon for those Apaches living around the Sierra Blanca mountains, a name probably derived from the Lipan Apache term for mescal people. The name Mescalero, the Spanish equivalent of the native term for people who ate the mescal plant, gradually replaced Natage during the last half of the eighteenth century.

The bulk of the Querechos of Coronado's era, later called Vaqueros and still later Vaquero Apaches, probably became the Lipan Apaches. Instead of following other Apache groups farther west and south into New Mexico, the Lipans seem to have shifted to the southeast into the Texas Panhandle. There they continued

Navajo summer shelter in Keams Canyon, Arizona.

SMITHSONIAN INSTITUTION, BUREAU OF AMERICAN ETHNOLOGY

to hunt buffalo and were sometimes joined on their hunts by Mescalero Apaches. They received little or no mention by the Spaniards until the late 1600s and early 1700s, probably because they had left the New Mexico settlements strictly alone until then.

This brings us to the final two Apache tribal divisions, the Jicarilla and Kiowa-Apache. These seem to have been the last Southern Athabascans to arrive in the Southwest, living on the plains to the north and northeast until the latter part of the seventeenth or early eighteenth centuries. The Jicarilla Apaches weren't mentioned by name by the Spaniards until 1700. They were given the name Jicarilla (Spanish for little basket) because of their expertness in making small basketry drinking cups. Archeologists have recently dug up sites in northeastern New Mexico where Jicarilla Apaches lived and farmed during the late 1600s. Like most Plains Apaches, they probably derived their farming skills from farming groups on the eastern plains, with the likely addition of certain elements picked up from trading and other close associations with the northern and eastern Pueblos.

But these weren't the only Southern Athabascans in the high plains country from Wyoming and Nebraska southward through Kansas and Colorado during the seventeenth century. There must have been quite a lot of them as the Spaniards called them by a welter of names which, in some cases, cannot now be associated with later Apache peoples.

There was even one Southern Athabascan group for which we have no recorded Spanish name, only that which archeologists have given them. These were the Dismal River peoples who farmed river valleys in western Nebraska and Kansas and northeastern Colorado between 1670 and 1723. Archeologists have found nearly a hundred of their small, semipermanent villages of grass or skin-covered lodges. These Plains Apaches were primarily hunters and gatherers, supplementing these foods by raising corn and squash. They made some utility pottery, and most of their stone and bone tools were those associated with hunting, butchering, and skin working.

An iron ax head found in the fireplace of a lodge at White Cat village in southwestern Nebraska showed that these Apaches had some contact, probably indirectly, with French or other Euro-

Large pottery jar of the Dismal River Culture dug up in a village site of these probable Southern Athabascan peoples in western Nebraska.

peans to the east. But occasional finds of turquoise, incised tubular pottery pipes, olivella shell beads, and glaze-painted pottery indicate considerable trade with the Pueblo Indians on the upper Rio Grande.

The Kiowa-Apaches, the last of the historic Southern Athabascan tribes in the Southwest, were originally Plains Apaches, perhaps one of the farming groups living up in Kansas or Colorado in the seventeenth century. Some time in the following century they gave up their farming and allied themselves with the Kiowas, perhaps because of their few numbers. The Kiowas, also a small tribe from Wyoming, spoke a language distantly related to Tanoan, one of the Pueblo languages. The Kiowa-Apaches took up the nomadic, buffalo-hunting life of the Kiowas but kept their own language and many of their own customs. Moving southward in the eighteenth century, the two tribes ended up east of the Jicarillas on the plains of southwestern Kansas and northwestern Oklahoma.

These, then, were the various divisions or groups of Southern Athabascan Indians at the time of the Spanish colonization of New Mexico. The entire history of the Apaches is closely linked to pressures from one side or another and subsequent shifts from plains to mountains to deserts and often back again. The ability of the Apaches to adapt to these pressures and new environments was an important factor in their survival.

The
Apache Wars

THE Apache Indian wrote his name in history with blood and fire and destruction. He was one of the first of the American Indians to fight back against the invading Europeans, and he was the last to give up the struggle. Asking no favors and giving none, he went down fighting.

The Apache Indian was a headache, a king-sized headache lasting nearly 300 years, to the armies of Spain, the Republic of Mexico, and the United States of America. He was also a headache to a lot of other Indian tribes in the Southwest. Leaders of these warring Southern Athabascans are legendary even today—Cochise, Geronimo, Victorio, Nana, Mangas Coloradas, Nachez, Loco, Chato, Chihuahua, Juh, Delegadito, Cuchillo, Diablo, Eskiminzin, Santana, Gomez, Manuelito, Ganado Mucho, Barboncito, Chacon, Lobo.

The conflict was not a continuous war. There were years of peace, during which considerable trading went on between the Apaches and Navajos and the Pueblo and other Indians, as well as between the Apaches and the Spaniards themselves. But during the seventeenth, eighteenth, and nineteenth centuries there were probably more years of warfare than there were of peace.

Nor did all of the Apache tribes go on the warpath at the same time. Some were raiding while others were trading with the enemy. It was normal practice for both Apaches and Spaniards or Mexicans to trade on one side of the mountains and loot and pillage on the other side.

This may seem odd, but the Apaches were not a nation, as the Spaniards so often referred to them. In fact, most Apache tribes wouldn't have even qualified as tribes in a strict political sense. Although each considered itself as one people, different from others, some tribes, like the Western Apaches, didn't have a name of their own to designate their entire tribe. Neither did the Chiricahuas. Most tribes didn't have a tribal chief, a tribal council, or a tribal government of any kind.

The typical Apache tribe was a loosely knit organization of a number of independent bands or groups, with no political ties or central leadership. In time, each band in a tribe became a self-sufficient unit and operated within a certain definite territory. Each band was usually made up of a number of smaller units called local groups, each of which was bound together by territorial association, blood, marriage, and personal friendship. Most such bands were relatively small, with probably not over 400 people in the biggest. Local groups were still smaller, ranging from 30 to 100 or so. Among the Western Apache and Chiricahua, for example, the local group was the basic social, economic, and military body. It was the largest unit that had a definite leader. If two or more local groups in a band got together for raiding or war, the most outstanding local group chief headed the combined group. Only rarely did an entire band unite for warfare or any other purpose. If they did, the most dominating of the local group chiefs became the head chief.

With this kind of political setup, it is easy to understand why there was no organized leadership for an entire band, let alone for the whole tribe. Yet most people can't imagine a tribe without a head chief. Neither could most of the Spanish, Mexican, and American officials, soldiers, and settlers in the Southwest. Treaties or other arrangements made with the chief of one local group were not binding on the chiefs of other local groups. One group might be at peace, another at war. Instead of dealing with one head chief, officials should have been dealing with twenty or thirty or more local group chiefs. Yet for centuries the Spaniards and later Mexicans and Americans continued to treat the various Apache divisions as distinct tribes, each ruled by a head chief.

It was not numbers that gave the Apaches their reputation. None of these seven Southern Athabascan tribes was ever very large, at least not until fairly recent times. At the begining of the seventeenth century, there were probably fewer than 10,000 Apaches and Navajos in and around the Southwest. These were split up into a dozen or more major tribal or geographic divisions and several times that many bands.

From the very beginning the Spaniards and the Pueblo Indians didn't get along. Coronado started the trouble. After struggling to feed and house his army and submitting to more and more overbearing demands, the Pueblo Indians finally rebelled. But they were no match for Spanish guns and armor and horses. Coronado quickly put down the revolt and had several hundred Indians executed as an object lesson.

These executions laid the groundwork for the mistrust and antagonism that thereafter characterized the relations between the Spaniards and the Pueblo Indians. In case the Indians had forgotten, Onate repeated the lesson sixty years later. The Indians of Acoma Pueblo had cleaned out their cupboards to supply one of Onate's exploring expeditions. A short time later a following expedition's demands for supplies were refused with the plea that the Indians could spare no more. The Spaniards attempted to take them by force and were beaten back, with the loss of their leader and a dozen or so soldiers. Onate retaliated by burning the pueblo and killing several hundred more Indians. Of those who survived, he ordered one foot cut off from each man over the age of twenty-five and imposed a fine of twenty years of personal servitude on each, with the same fine for all men between twelve and twenty-five and for all women over twelve years of age. Onate considered this a warning to the other Pueblo Indians that rebellious acts of any kind would be dealt with promptly and severely.

The Pueblo Indians, along with the rest of the southwestern tribes, weren't prepared for the impact of European peoples and their foreign culture with their metal tools, wheeled vehicles, firearms, horses, sheep, and other domestic animals, and, equally important, a new religion that tolerated no competing rituals or beliefs. Much of this was beyond the comprehension of most Indian groups. Heretofore, the Pueblo Indians had met other Indians more or less as equals. Now they were meeting white-faced strangers who looked down on them as inferiors, as conquered peoples, to be treated as servants, slaves, or subjects.

The Spaniards, from soldiers to settlers and missionaries, ruthlessly exploited the Indians. Captive in their villages, the Pueblo Indians became the Spaniards' main source of supply. Not only did the Indians have to pay tribute (taxes) in corn and cloth, they also had to work for little or nothing for their new overlords. Most officials had come to the New World with only one thought in mind—to get rich as quickly as possible. They put Indians to work weaving cloth and blankets, making wagons, building houses, herding cattle and sheep, tilling farms, and gathering pinyon nuts and anything else that could be sold at a profit in Mexico. Settlers wanted free Indian labor to build houses and work their fields. Each soldier was entitled to a tract of land and the services of a number of Indians. Missionaries began a monumental building program, with churches in larger pueblos and chapels in smaller ones, all, of course, built with Indian labor. While these mission compounds were supposed to be training centers for Indians, they became workshops where Indians were employed at weaving, blacksmithing, and leatherworking, and as cooks and servants. Other Indians herded the missions' cattle and sheep and took care of the missions' gardens and orchards.

The missionaries tried to convert the heathen Indians into good Christians, chiefly by stamping out native religious customs and beliefs and forcibly imposing their own Christian ideas and practices. Periodically they raided the village ceremonial centers, the kivas, and burned masks and prayer sticks and other sacred Indian objects. Pueblo religious leaders were whipped and even hanged as witches if they persisted in their ceremonies. Failure to attend church services was considered a crime, and offenders were dealt with severely.

All these drastic disciplinary measures against native beliefs and practices merely served to swell Indian resentment against the

The ruins of the seventeenth-century Franciscan church at Gran Quivira National Monument, New Mexico.

Spaniards. They did not give up their beliefs or even their sacred rites. Ostensibly, they went along with the missionaries, but they still continued to follow their own religious rituals and beliefs in secret.

Added to the troubles of the Pueblo Indians in the early 1600s were the increasing raids by nomadic Indian tribes, chiefly the Apaches. Most of the first Spanish accounts tell not of raids but of trading among the Pueblo Indians and Spaniards and the Apaches. That situation, however, didn't last long. Nomadic or seminomadic tribes, such as the Apaches were then, had been periodically raiding Indian farming villages for about as long as there had been farmers and nomads. The Spaniards may have caught the first Plains Apaches in one of their trading moods. But the Apaches were soon back in the raiding business against both Spaniards and their reluctant hosts, the Pueblo Indians.

One reason for the renewed attacks may lie in Spanish slave-hunting practices. The Spaniards in northern Mexico had been expanding their mines and ranches so fast that there were not enough local Indian slaves to work these new developments. Now bands of slavers were looking to the north for more captives. Even though Spanish law said that only Indians captured in warfare could be held as slaves, it was always easy to start a war.

THE APACHE WARS   39

The Spaniards early recognized that most Indian tribes were fiercely independent and unwilling to join together to fight a common enemy. So the Spanish policy was to pit one Indian tribe against another. Thus they encouraged some Apache tribes to raid other southwestern or Plains Indian tribes to obtain captives which the Indians could exchange for corn, blankets, and steel knives. Nor were the Spaniards above treacherously attacking a friendly Apache band and taking prisoners to be sent to Mexico as slaves. From Spanish records we know that one such incident happened on the plains in 1637. Most Spanish governors captured Apaches to be sold as slaves in the mining camps of northern Mexico. In 1662 one Spanish governor claimed that he had an interest in some ninety Apache slaves. The Apaches retaliated the only way they knew how, by raiding and killing and taking captives of their own.

In 1606 either Navajos or Plains Apaches raided the Spanish settlement of San Gabriel on the upper Rio Grande. The Spaniards immediately sent out a force against the marauding Apaches, and the war was on. From that time on the various Apache groups were intermittently at war with the Spaniards and the Pueblo Indians.

Apache and Navajo raids and wars over the next two centuries were too numerous to list. We can only touch on their highlights and on the movements of Apache bands and tribes and other southwestern Indians from one location to another and note the results of these shifts in population.

As early as 1630 Fray Alonso Benavides, one of the Spanish missionaries, was describing the Apaches, particularly the Navajos, as a vast group of very numerous and very dangerous enemies entirely surrounding New Mexico. This was probably pure propaganda, highly exaggerated in an endeavor to secure more priests and soldiers for the new colony.

There was no doubt, however, that Apache raids were increasing. Between the 1630s and 1660s most Apaches and Navajos had stolen or traded for enough horses to put everyone in the tribes on horseback. More mobile now, they were able to strike fast and get away equally fast. They took anything that wasn't nailed down—food, clothing, blankets, jewelry, weapons, horses, mules, cattle, sheep, and women and small children. In 1669 one Spanish writer

Pueblo Indian woman and children in front of a Rio Grande Indian village.

reported that no road was safe from attack by the heathen Apache.

Nor had time improved relations between the Pueblo Indians and the Spaniards. Missionaries were still trying to wipe out native rituals by whipping or selling into slavery or hanging Indians who wouldn't give up their religion. Each new governor, and there were a lot of them, seemed to impose heavier taxes of corn and cotton cloth. From 1640 to 1679 there were half a dozen different Pueblo revolts against their masters. But only a few towns took part at any one time, and the Spaniards were easily able to subdue them.

Then came 1680 and what has been called the First American Revolution. For the only time in their history virtually all of the Pueblo Indians united together in a common cause: to drive all of the Spaniards out of the Southwest. Even the distant Hopi and Zuni Indians joined in the uprising. Under the leadership of Pope, a Tewa medicine man from San Juan Pueblo, bows and arrows finally won out over guns and armor. Within three weeks 21 missionaries and nearly 400 Spanish soldiers and settlers had been killed and the surviving 2,000 colonists driven far south to what is now El Paso. The Indians celebrated their victory by tearing down the churches and missions, burning their furnishings and records, and wiping out all other signs of the hated Spaniards.

Once the Spaniards had been booted out, the Pueblo villages returned to their old way of life. Pope tried to keep them united, but the independent Indians would have nothing to do with it and went back to being individual towns again. In 1692–93 the Spaniards returned in force and, although some of the villages resisted, by 1696 the Spaniards were once more in full control of the area.

There was one Pueblo area the Spaniards never reconquered. That was the Hopi country in northern Arizona. Only at their easternmost town, Awatovi, were missionaries allowed back to rebuild their church. However, so strong was the Hopi feeling against the Spaniards and their religion that in 1700 warriors from the other Hopi towns sacked Awatovi, killing the men and distributing the women and children among the various towns. Awatovi was completely demolished and was never again rebuilt or reoccupied. Several times the Spaniards tried to return, but each time the Hopis sent them packing.

The rebellion had, however, been even harder on the Pueblo Indians than it had on the Spaniards. Since the early 1600s scores of towns had been abandoned, and the Pueblo population had been practically cut in half as a result of periodic smallpox epidemics, Apache raids, and deaths at the hands of the Spaniards. Beginning in the 1670s both Navajos and Apaches had taken advantage of the situation by raiding the Pueblo villages for food and livestock. They had steered clear of allying themselves with either side during the Pueblo rebellion and after the reconquest kept right on raiding Spanish and Pueblo settlements alike. To escape brutal Spanish reprisals during the last years of the seventeenth century and the first decades of the eighteenth, large numbers of Pueblo Indians fled to the Navajo country and to the distant Hopi villages.

This was a crucial period for the Navajos. Over the next fifty years they radically changed their way of life as they absorbed Pueblo technology and ideas: techniques of farming, care of live-

Hopi Indian bowl made by the celebrated potter, Nampeo. TAD NICHOLS

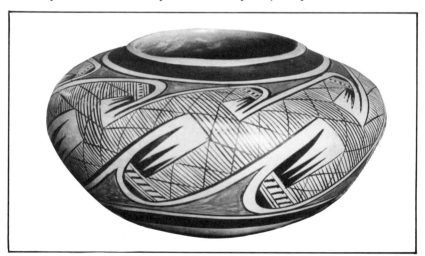

stock, pottery making, and weaving, and such religious and social concepts as prayer sticks, ceremonial masks, altars, sand paintings, and probably the Pueblo matrilineal clan system.

Spanish missionaries had better luck in southern Arizona. In the 1690s Jesuit missionaries moved down the San Pedro and Santa Cruz Rivers into Arizona from Sonora. But they never got too far north. By the time they had established half a dozen missions, the one farthest north being located just south of what was later to become Tucson, the Apaches were giving them fits.

All during the seventeenth century the Gila Apaches had been consolidating their hold on western New Mexico. They had split up into about half a dozen groups and had spread out until they covered most of the territory west of the Rio Grande from the Pueblo country on the north southward almost to the Mexican border. They had begun raiding Zuni, Acoma, Laguna, and other Pueblo towns and had harassed Spanish caravans moving up and down the wagon road connecting El Paso and Santa Fe. By the 1680s and 1690s they were raiding southward into Chihuahua and Sonora. By the early 1700s some of these Gila Apaches had migrated westward into the then uninhabited high mountain country of eastern Arizona, while others went into southeastern Arizona. Here they formed an effective barrier between the Spaniards in northern New Mexico and their newly arrived cousins in southern Arizona and northern Sonora. Over the next century those Gila Apaches in eastern Arizona gradually differentiated from their neighboring relatives and became known as the Coyotero Apaches or White Mountain Apaches (the Western Apaches of today), with those in southeastern Arizona becoming the Chiricahuas.

About this same time the Apaches out on the plains suddenly found themselves up to their necks in trouble. The Comanches were on the loose.

The Comanches had been one of a number of nomadic Shoshonean-speaking tribes in southern Wyoming making a living by hunting and gathering. With the opening of the eighteenth century, however, they began getting horses from the south and expanding their range southward toward the source of supply. By 1706 the Spaniards first mentioned the Comanches by name as being in southeastern Colorado. Within a short time the Comanches had picked up still more horses and were rapidly becoming known as the finest horsemen of the plains. Raiding Indian and white settlements alike, the Comanches fell with telling effect on the scattered and relatively unprotected Apache communities on the northern and eastern borders of the Southwest.

The southward march of the Comanches was probably the reason why the Jicarilla Apaches left the plains country and moved into northern New Mexico. Comanche pressure also seemingly forced other Plains Apaches—the Cuartelejos, Carlanas, Palomas, and Chipaynes—to ally themselves with the Jicarillas. All of these five Apache groups, possibly along with one or two more so far unidentified Plains Apache peoples, were apparently separate divisions yet still living together until 1754. After that date Spanish reports referred to them all as Jicarillas.

While some Comanches stayed in southern Colorado and, along with the neighboring Utes to the west, continued harassing the Jicarilla and northern Pueblo and Spanish communities, other Comanches shifted to the southeast into Oklahoma and the Texas Panhandle. From there they continued to raid the Spanish and Indian settlements in the Pueblo country and were in turn attacked by the Spaniards in 1717. In 1723 the Comanches defeated the Lipan Apaches and forced them to retreat still further south in Texas.

Within a few decades the Comanches had accomplished something the Spaniards had been unable to do in nearly 150 years. These swift-moving horsemen had broken the Apache domination of the high plains, driving them out of southeastern Colorado, extreme eastern New Mexico, and northern Texas. This didn't help the Spaniards any, however, as they had just exchanged one band of raiders for another. By the second quarter of the eighteenth century, the Comanches were in full control of the plains east of New Mexico, from which region they were a constant threat for the next 150 years.

In 1743 the Comanches again defeated the Lipans and drove them deeper into Texas, where they finally sought protection from the Spaniards around San Antonio. In the 1750s and 1760s the Spaniards established several missions for the Lipans in south Texas. But, under repeated attacks by Comanches and other plains tribes, the missions were soon abandoned, and many Lipans fled to south

Texas and across the Rio Grande into Coahuila in northern Mexico.

Like the Lipans, the Mescalero Apaches were caught between pressures of the Spaniards in New Mexico and the Comanches to the east. When the Mescaleros went buffalo hunting on the plains, they usually joined bands of Lipan Apaches as a security measure against the Comanches. The Spaniards even gave the name Llanero to these two Apache groups when they were hunting buffalo on the plains. But this changed when the Comanches chased the Lipans clear across Texas into Mexico. Then the Comanches went after the Mescaleros. So did the Spaniards in New Mexico. In 1776 a Spanish expedition forced the Mescaleros out of their homeland in the Sierra Blancas into the eastern plains in Texas, where the Comanches promptly fell on them and chased them back home. In 1786 the Comanches came into eastern New Mexico and cleaned the Mescaleros out of the east side of the Sierra Blancas. In that same year the Spaniards finally succeeded in making peace with the Comanches. But the Comanches continued to fight against the Mescaleros and Utes and other Indians on the borders of what they claimed to be their territory. Directly to their north, however, they did have friendly neighbors, where the Kiowas and Kiowa-Apaches had settled after following the Comanches south from Wyoming. When the Mescaleros couldn't get into the plains to hunt buffalo, they turned their attention to the Spanish flocks of sheep and herds of cattle and horses in New Mexico.

Their relatives in western New Mexico and eastern Arizona, the Western Apaches and Navajos and various Chiricahua and other groups of Gila Apaches, were already doing exactly the same thing. In fact, nearly everybody in the Southwest was taking a crack at the Spaniards and Mexicans on both sides of the border. Even the relatively peaceful Pimas and Papagos in northern Sonora and southern Arizona briefly rebelled against their overlords in 1751. One result of this was the establishment the following year of a Spanish presidio (military post) at Tubac in southern Arizona. Twenty-four years later a second presidio was founded at Tucson. But the presence of these posts and their garrisons of soldiers didn't stop Apache raids.

By the middle of the eighteenth century the Spaniards had established settlements northward throughout Sonora and Chihuahua to the present United States border. Twin prongs of civilization ran up the Rio Grande valley to northern New Mexico and down the Santa Cruz and San Pedro valleys into southern Arizona. Contrary to the course of most rivers, these last two run north. Over this area there was a widely scattered Spanish and Mexican and native Indian population in presidios, missions, towns, mining camps, and ranches.

This was an ideal situation for the Apaches, and they took full advantage of it. For the next 140-odd years raiding in Mexico after plunder was a fixed part of the Apache way of life. They stole horses, mules, cattle, women and children for slaves, and anything else that could be transported northward.

The size of the territory in Sonora and Chihuahua over which they raided is extraordinary. They knew the country south of the border as well as they did their own. Every mountain and spring and town had its Apache name. Raiding parties sometimes even reached the Gulf of California. Several northern Mexican towns suffered so heavily from Apache raids that many ranches and missions and towns themselves had to be abandoned.

Many Spaniards and Mexicans even secretly encouraged Apache raiding. What was stolen from one town or mining camp found ready sale in another a few hundred miles away. Horses and mules rounded up in raids in Sonora and Chihuahua were frequently trailed north and traded to Spaniards and Mexicans in Santa Fe and other New Mexico towns. Just as frequently the Apaches would turn right around, steal other horses and mules in New Mexico, and take them south to sell in Mexico. Some Sonora and Chihuahua towns flourished on trade in stolen goods.

During the 1770s, 1780s, and 1790s, Apache raiding along the border became so serious that the Spanish officials carried out a series of intensive campaigns against several groups of Apaches in southern Arizona and New Mexico. They killed a number and captured a few more to be sold as slaves. But about all they actually accomplished was temporary interruptions in the raids. Within a few months the Apaches were back at their favorite pastime again. Time and time again they attacked Spanish caravans passing up and down the Rio Grande and even raided El Paso itself. In 1776 Apaches ran off some 500 animals from Tubac,

Zuni Pueblo Indian woman carrying water in a jar on her head.

AMERICAN MUSEUM OF NATURAL HISTORY

leaving the entire garrison literally on foot. Over the next two decades bands of Apaches raided all the way from Acoma and Laguna Pueblos in the north to Spanish ranches and settlements hundreds of miles to the south. Try as hard as they might, the Spaniards were unable to subdue the Apaches.

In fact, the various groups of Apaches—the Navajos, Western Apaches, Gila Apaches, Chiricahuas, Mescaleros, Jicarillas, and Lipans—formed a barrier across Arizona and New Mexico and western Texas which effectively kept the Spaniards bottled up in the Southwest. If the Spaniards had ever had any thought about expanding their colonization efforts northward, they soon forgot about it. They already had more than they could handle.

The Spaniards in New Mexico also had a new menace rapidly closing in on their northern and eastern frontiers. The sale of the vast and as yet poorly defined Louisiana Territory by France to the United States in 1803 brought the Spaniards new neighbors— the Americans. Within a few years of the sale the first American traders began appearing in Santa Fe.

Around the opening of the nineteenth century the Spaniards finally came up with a new approach in their efforts to pacify the Apaches. Their reasoning ran like this: a hungry Apache was a raiding Apache, while a well-fed one might stay at home. So they began supplying some of the Apaches with gifts and regular rations. This policy worked after a fashion. As long as the Indians received their gifts and rations, they remained relatively peaceful.

This situation didn't last too long, however. In 1810 the Mexicans began their own revolution to gain independence from Spain. The Spaniards immediately withdrew most of their troops from the northern frontier to fight the rebels far to the south. The much smaller garrisons that remained could no longer control, much less supply, those Apaches who were at peace. When their gifts and rations were cut off, the Apaches went back to raiding as the second best way of making a living. With too few soldiers to stop them, the Apaches forced the abandonment of mines, missions, ranches, and settlements all over the Southwest.

In 1821 the Mexicans finally won in their struggle for independence from Spain. But the change in flags brought no change in policy that aided the Apaches or other southwestern Indians.

If there was any difference between a Spaniard and a Mexican, the Apaches were unable to find it. Nearly three centuries of contact had served only to increase the hostility between Indians and Spaniards and Mexicans. The Mexicans, if anything, were even more determined than the Spaniards to put an end to the Apache problem in either of two ways: by taking captives to be sold as slaves or by killing all those Apaches who refused to surrender.

But the Apaches kept right on raiding and looting and killing. By 1835 conditions had become so bad, with a reported 5,000 Mexicans killed or taken captive in the preceding fifteen years, that the Sonoran government inaugurated its own Apache pacification program. Apache scalps would be paid for at the scale of 100 pesos (a peso being about the equivalent of a dollar) for the scalp of an adult male Apache, 50 pesos for the scalp of an adult female, and 25 pesos for the scalp of a child. Two years later the state of Chihuahua adopted a similar reward system for Apache scalps.

Within a short time bands of bounty hunters were combing Apacheria for Apache Indians to scalp. Many of these were Americans—traders, trappers, miners, mountain men—who had been steadily moving into Spanish territory to make their fortunes. There were even eastern Indians among these scalp hunters— Shawnee, Delaware, and Creek guides and trappers who had come west to work for various fur companies.

Some of these Americans had been in Spanish territory for a decade or more, trapping beaver along the Gila River and mining at the Mexican copper mines at Santa Rita in southern New Mexico. The several Gila Apache groups had treated these first Americans —white eyes as they called them—in a friendly manner, even though many of these early mountain men were anything but friendly. The Apaches' enemies, so they thought, were the Mexicans, not this handful of strange-looking men who spoke a foreign tongue and who seemed unlikely to take up permanent residence in Apacheria. Time would show the Apaches how wrong they were.

That time wasn't long in coming. In 1837 James Johnson, an American trader in Sonora, accepted the Mexican government's offer of a large reward for the scalp of Juan Jose, chief of the Copper Mine band of Apaches near Santa Rita, New Mexico.

Johnson and Juan Jose were good friends, Juan Jose having used Johnson's trading post as a safe and profitable outlet for the disposal of surplus booty secured in raids. Gathering a small party of Americans, Johnson took a pack train to Santa Rita and sent word to Juan Jose that he had brought gifts and food for him and his people. Naturally, Juan Jose and some thirty Apache men, women, and children showed up for the affair. When the Indians crowded closely around the pile of food, Johnson fired a hidden cannon, killing Juan Jose and more than twenty other Apaches. Johnson lost no time in collecting the scalps from his victims. Apache raiders destroyed Johnson's trading post, but Johnson managed to elude his attackers and escape to Mexico. Not so fortunate were other American traders and trappers in New Mexico. Mangas Coloradas (Red Sleeves) assumed the leadership of the Copper Mine Apaches and took revenge for Johnson's treacherous attack by killing twenty-two Americans trapping on the Gila River.

Similar events were happening down in Sonora and Chihuahua. Some scalp hunters, like the Americans James Kirker and John Glanton, reportedly collected up to 30,000 or 40,000 dollars for

Navajo country in the Four Corners area, where Arizona, New Mexico, Colorado, and Utah meet.

Apache scalps. But more of them weren't so successful. After all, there had scarcely been a day during the past two centuries when somebody was not scheming to run the Apache out of his country or make a dead Indian out of him, and consequently most Apaches just weren't that easy to catch. Many bounty hunters probably lost their own scalps while they were still trying to ambush their first Indian, as the Apaches, infuriated by the actions of these hunters, intensified their raiding and killing.

Scalp hunters soon found that it was far safer to scalp friendly farming Indians, like the Pima and Opota. To the Mexican authorities one Indian's hair looked just like the hair of any other Indian. But the hunters put themselves out of business when they became too greedy and began mixing black Mexican tresses with those of the Indians. This was too much for the Mexicans, and the American scalp hunters were lucky to escape with their own hair still intact.

Over the next half a dozen years things didn't change much on the Arizona and New Mexico frontier. More Americans kept moving into the territory as political relations between the United States and Mexico became more and more critical. And the Apaches kept right on raiding as they had always been doing.

By now the Apaches were in the final stages of consolidating into definite tribes or tribal bands and were concentrating in those areas where we generally find them today. Most of them were called by the names by which we now know them.

The Navajos, who had been expanding to the south and west since the mid 1700s, had moved into eastern and northeastern Arizona and spread over into southeastern Utah. The four or five bands of Plains farming and hunting Apaches who had joined forces with the Jicarillas a century earlier to get out of the path of the Comanches now formed a single tribal unit, the Jicarilla Apaches. They were still living in the mountains on the east side of the Rio Grande in northern New Mexico, next-door neighbors to the Pueblo Indians. The Kiowa-Apaches, still tagging along with the Kiowas, were out on the plains of Oklahoma north of the Comanches. What few hundred Lipan Apaches were left were far down in Texas and northern Coahuila, while the Mescalero

Apaches ranged from the mountains of southern New Mexico east of the Rio Grande on down into west Texas.

The Western Apaches, called by such primarily geographic names as San Carlos Apaches, Coyotero Apaches, White Mountain Apaches, or Tonto Apaches, were still living in the mountainous country of east-central Arizona. To the south, in and around the Chiricahua Mountains of southeastern Arizona, were the Chiricahua Apaches. Still farther to the south in the Sierra Madre Mountains of northern Mexico was a separate band of Chiricahuas known as the Southern Chiricahua Apaches. Over in southwestern New Mexico lived the several groups or bands of what had been termed, and still often were, the Gila Apaches— Mogollon, Copper Mines, Mimbres, and Warm Springs Apaches. That was the situation in the Southwest in 1846 when war broke out, a war not between Apaches and Mexicans or Americans, but a war between Mexicans and Americans following the annexation of the Republic of Texas to the United States in 1845.

The Coming
of the
White Eyes

THE final dramatic act of the Apache Indians' struggle for freedom began with the signing of the Treaty of Guadalupe Hidalgo in 1848. With that, the United States took over all of Apacheria north of the Gila River. Five years later, in 1853, the Gadsden Purchase gave the United States the responsibility for the rest of Apache territory as far south as the present international boundary.

For over 200 years the Spaniards had tried in vain to subdue the stubborn Apaches. The Mexicans had little better luck in their short quarter of a century rule. Now it was the Americans' turn, and it took them nearly 40 years to accomplish the trick.

When the long military columns and creaking supply wagons of the United States army began rolling into the Southwest, the Apaches were pleased. They thought these newcomers, the White Eyes, would chase out the hated Mexicans, and Apache life would be better. Consequently, they kept a watchful eye on the rolling guns and lines of soldiers but gave them little trouble. This wasn't the Apaches' war. Let the Americans and Mexicans fight it out far to the south in Mexico.

But once in a while temptation proved too much to resist, and a few horses and mules and other supplies would vanish under cover of darkness. Yet seldom did the American troops have any more success than had the Mexicans in overtaking and punishing Apache raiders. Usually no Apache thieves were captured and no animals were recovered.

But this relatively peaceful interlude didn't last long after the signing of the peace treaty with Mexico. According to Article 11 of the treaty, the United States government was supposed to keep their new wards, the Apaches and other southwestern Indians, at home north of the border. If any did stray south on raids, the United States was supposed to punish the offenders and to pay the Mexicans for losses inflicted by these Indian marauders.

This, of course, was a difficult, if not impossible, task. The new boundary line meant nothing to the Apaches. As yet, it hadn't even shown up on the ground as a physical boundary. For over 150 years raiding into Sonora, Chihuahua, and Coahuila was a regular part of their lives. They couldn't understand why now all of a sudden they should stop. Weren't the Mexicans still their enemies? Besides, if they didn't raid in Mexico—running off horses and mules and cattle, taking anything portable, kidnaping women and children, killing the men—how would they themselves manage to live? That was a good question, one that seemingly had no answer. At least, the United States government couldn't come up with any.

As to that part of the treaty about punishing the offenders, first they had to be caught. That was also a difficult task, as the United States army was to learn.

Typical of Apache tactics was a raid in 1850 by a small group of Gila Apaches on a little town on the Rio Grande north of El Paso. After a brief skirmish in which the raiders killed one man and wounded several others, they took off to the east. The United States cavalry from Fort Bliss soon arrived and set out in hot pursuit of the Indians. While the troops were hunting for them on the plains to the east, the Apaches scattered and circled back to the river. There they joined forces and again raided the town and stole all the livestock, escaping into the mountains to the west with the animals.

Nor did the Americans chase out the hated Mexicans, as the

Apaches had thought they would do. Instead, they protected the Mexicans in New Mexico because they had now become American citizens. The Apaches and Navajos and other southwestern Indians weren't American citizens because under federal law, which wouldn't be changed for many years, Indians were held to be foreigners, their tribes foreign nations to be dealt with only by treaty. The Indians, the only truly native-born Americans, were classed as foreigners in their own country.

Over the next few years of the 1850s the Americans had plenty of trouble with bands of Apaches raiding across the border into Mexico. Year by year the Mexican claims for losses sustained as a result of these raids mounted higher and higher into the millions of dollars. Finally, in 1853, the United States signed an agreement, the Gadsden Purchase, with Mexico. For 10 million dollars Article 11 of the Guadalupe Hidalgo peace treaty was abolished, and the United States got the lands it wanted in southern New Mexico and Arizona to the present border. All this meant to the Apaches was that the international boundary had been moved a few miles farther south. They couldn't have cared less; the border had never meant anything to them.

The Americans were also hard pressed to cope with the problem of protecting American settlers and traders, Mexican ranchers, and Pueblo Indians from raids by Jicarillas, Utes, Navajos, Gila Apaches, and Plains Indians in northern New Mexico both east and west of the Rio Grande. During one five-year period in the 1850s, official records indicate that Navajos and Apaches made off with an estimated 450,000 sheep, 32,000 cattle, 13,000 mules, and 7,000 horses from northern New Mexico ranches and towns.

The Jicarillas, provoked by an unwarranted assault by a group of soldiers, began attacking wagon trains between Taos and Santa Fe, on one occasion killing eleven men carrying mail, on another capturing a woman and child who were later murdered. New Mexico's first Indian agent, James Calhoun, eventually persuaded the Jicarillas to sign a peace treaty giving them farm lands and rations. Calhoun sent the treaty on to Washington. That was the last that was ever heard of it. When the rations and farming equipment didn't turn up, the Jicarillas promptly went back on the warpath. In 1854 Jicarillas and Utes swept down on Pueblo, Col-

Issue of rations to Navajo Indians in 1879.
SMITHSONIAN INSTITUTION, BUREAU OF AMERICAN ETHNOLOGY

orado, killing 15 men, abducting women and children, and stealing 200 head of livestock. Hard pressed by the army, the Jicarillas sued for peace in 1855 and were put on a reservation in northeastern New Mexico. But this was sold out from under them. Over the next thirty years they were moved from one place to another as first one agency and then another tried to find a place for them to settle. Reservations were granted and soon cancelled. Rations were given and then suspended. Finally, in 1887, they were given a reservation in northern New Mexico, and there they still are today. This was typical of the way the United States army and various governmental officials and agencies handled—or, rather, mishandled—most problems dealing with the Indians.

There was no such thing as a consistent Indian policy. One Indian agent played the game by one set of rules, the next by a new set, while the military played by a still different set. One Indian commissioner would recommend one solution to the Indian problem, his successor still another. Decisions about Indians were usually shaped more by politics than justice.

The Indians of this new frontier territory were relatively unknown to the Americans. Tribal distinctions among Indians were often confusing to Americans who were without the benefit of Spanish intelligence on this subject. The Americans had to learn the hard way that, while most Indians looked alike, their politics and behavior might differ. The fact that an Apache tribe was a loosely knit organization of independent bands, each more or less under its own leader, caused a great deal of misunderstanding. Time after time army or civilian officials negotiated an agreement or treaty with an Apache leader, expecting him to be acting for all his people. They didn't realize that he could speak only for his own band and only for such of them as chose to go along with him. Indians who had signed no agreements and made no promises could never understand why they should be punished for violating treaties which had been made without their knowledge and consent.

There was an almost complete lack of understanding between the Americans and the Apaches. The two were completely opposite in their system of values. By and large the Americans were thrifty and industrious. They were eager to acquire money and property and were generally willing to work hard to get it. To them time was important. To the Apaches time meant nothing. They cared little for personal property or work. The white people thought the Indians were lazy and shiftless, while the Indians thought the white people worked themselves to death. It is no wonder that the Indians and Americans were continually at odds.

The years between 1855 and 1861 were up and down years for the Apaches. In New Mexico Indian agents were appointed for some of the Indian tribes, like the Mescalero Apaches. Some of the Gila Apaches and Mescaleros signed peace treaties and were given a few implements and some seed and encouraged to plant crops. But to most Americans, soldiers and civilians alike, one Indian was just like any other Indian, and the only good Indian was a dead Indian.

The Mescalero Apaches soon found this out. They had tried to become farmers, but inhabitants of neighboring settlements didn't want Indians around anywhere, peaceful or not. Some of these settlers organized raids against small Mescalero camps, slaying some thirty men, women, and children. After the second such massacre, thirty-seven of the raiders were arrested by the army, but they were soon turned loose on the demands of civil officials. None of them was ever brought to trial or punished. Nobody was ever punished for killing an Indian.

Mangas Coloradas, chief of the Copper Mine Apaches, also got a taste of white man's justice. Gold had been discovered in western New Mexico in the 1850s, and miners flooded into the area. Mangas Coloradas didn't like having that many Americans in the heart of Apacheria. He tried to induce them to leave by promising to guide them to an even bigger gold mine to the south. He probably knew what he was talking about, but the miners were suspicious of his good intentions. They tied him up, whipped him, and then turned him loose. There was no greater insult to an Apache chief. Mangas Coloradas never forgot that whipping and wasted no time in wiping out the outrage in blood.

While the Chiricahua Apaches had been raiding in Mexico, they had left the relatively few Americans in southern Arizona more or less alone. Perhaps this was because the Americans had not tried to set up permanent settlements in Chiricahua territory. Or perhaps it was because of the far-sighted wisdom of the great

Chiricahua leader, Cochise. In 1858 Cochise gave permission to the Butterfield Stage Company to run a stage line across Chiricahua territory and to build a stage station near the spring at Apache Pass at the northern end of the Chiricahua Mountains. Cochise kept his word, and stages began operating between New Mexico and Tucson without interference from the Indians. Cochise contracted to supply the station with wood and even protected it against attacks by renegade Apaches, killing at least four of the Indians.

That peaceful situation came to an end in 1861, not, however, through any fault of Cochise's. Late in the preceding year a party of Apaches, possibly Pinal Apaches (Western Apaches) raided south of Patagonia, Arizona, kidnaping a small boy and stealing a herd of cattle. Acting on the erroneous belief that the raiders had been Chiricahuas, the commanding officer of Fort Buchanan, the only army post at that time in Arizona, finally sent a detachment of troops to the stage station in Apache Pass. In command was a young lieutenant, George Bascom, fresh out of West Point. Bascom didn't know Indians, yet he instinctively felt that all Indians were bad. Arriving at the station, Bascom demanded that Cochise return the boy and the cattle. He refused to listen to Cochise's denial of knowledge of the boy or the cattle and, despite the fact that the Apaches were there under a flag of truce, he tried to arrest Cochise and half a dozen of his followers. Historians differ widely on just what happened next. Whatever the true story, Cochise himself escaped and captured a number of American hostages, offering to exchange them for his own people still held prisoner. Bascom refused, and Cochise eventually killed the six hostages he held, while the army hanged six Apaches, including Cochise's brother and two of his nephews. These acts of treachery toward both Cochise and Mangas Coloradas brought a new wave of death and destruction across Arizona and New Mexico.

About the same time the War between the States broke out, and many of the troops were withdrawn from the Southwest. All the Apaches knew was that Americans were killing other Americans, both in New Mexico and far off to the east. Cochise and Mangas Coloradas gathered their warriors together and began raiding ranches and mining camps and settlements. Many of the outlying ranches and mining camps were abandoned as their inhabitants sought refuge in Tucson and Mesilla and other towns.

The biggest battle ever fought between Apaches and Americans occurred in July 1862. United States troops on their way from Tucson to New Mexico were attacked in Apache Pass by a combined force of Chiricahua and Gila Apaches under Cochise and Mangas Coloradas. As a prelude to the battle, Mangas and his warriors ambushed and slaughtered a party of fourteen miners coming from the east. Cochise and his Indians had built stone breastworks on the hills above the springs. In an ordinary battle these might have won out for the Indians. However, when the troops brought up two howitzers, the ear-shattering reports of the cannon and the explosive shells proved too much for the Indians. Mangas Coloradas was wounded and was taken by his men to the town of Janos, Chihuahua, where a Mexican doctor, under threat of his own death and those in the town, saved his life.

But Mangas Coloradas had nearly reached the end of his seventy-odd years. With age came a desire for peace. In January 1863 through an offer of peace and under a flag of truce, he was tricked into an army camp in New Mexico and murdered. The army immediately began other campaigns against the southern Apaches.

At the same time another intensive campaign was under way against the Navajos. When the American army marched into Santa Fe in August 1846, their first troubles came not from the Mexicans but from the Navajos. Less than a month later the Navajos raided General Kearny's cattle herd, along with the sheep and horse herds of neighboring settlements. General Kearny sent out an expedition to meet with the Navajos. Fourteen Navajo leaders signed a treaty and exchanged gifts with the officers. Within a few days the Navajos resumed their raids. That set the pattern for the next fifteen years—raids, signing of treaties, exchange of gifts, and then more raids.

Finally, in 1852, Fort Defiance was established in the heart of Navajo country, and for a few years there was relative peace. But by 1860 there were fifteen companies of troops waging an active campaign against the Navajos. These were withdrawn as soon as war broke out the following year in the East. The Navajos were

Three Navajo chiefs in 1874. From left to right, Ganado Mucho (Much Cattle), chief of a band; Tiene-su-se, third war chief; and Mariana, second war chief.

quick to take advantage of the army's absence and increased their raids upon Rio Grande settlements.

By 1862, however, General James H. Carleton's 1,500 California troops, having chased the Confederate forces back into Texas, were tired of building roads and doing housekeeping chores around army posts. They wanted action, someone to fight. General Carleton gave it to them—war with the Mescalero Apaches and Navajos. First he began an all-out campaign against the Mescaleros, with orders to kill all Mescalero men and put the captive women and children on a reservation at newly established Fort Sumner on the Pecos River in east-central New Mexico. By the middle of 1863 Colonel Kit Carson, former mountain man, and his troops had imprisoned over 400 Mescaleros at Fort Sumner. Many others moved south into Mexico, while some went to live with Apache groups west of the Rio Grande.

Kit Carson then turned his troops loose on the Navajos. The Navajos had become the biggest Southern Athabascan tribe in the Southwest, numbering an estimated 13,000. Their redrock country was spectacularly scenic, but it was also big and rugged. Carson knew he had a tough job ahead of him. He had a new fort, Fort Wingate, built on the southern edge of Navajo country. He gave the Navajos until July 20, 1863, to surrender peacefully and be taken to Fort Sumner, after which date he would shoot the men who resisted, capture the women and children, destroy the crops, and take the sheep. He enlisted the aid of Utes and Mexicans, who were offered 20 dollars for every Navajo horse and 1 dollar for every Navajo sheep turned in to the army. He was also helped by numerous bands of heavily armed New Mexicans and Ute Indians intent upon capturing Navajo women and children to be sold as slaves.

Although the Navajos outnumbered Carson's troops, they had few guns and less gunpowder and lead and were no military match for the United States army. But Carson didn't fight the Navajos in the usual manner. Dividing his command into small parties, he began a scorched earth policy: they burned every hogan, every planted field, every storehouse; chopped down the hundreds of peach trees that Navajos had obtained from the Spaniards; and killed or rounded up Navajo horses, cattle, and sheep.

When Carson continued his campaign into the winter, it was too much for the Navajos. Many of the older people and women and children had already died of hunger or exposure, and the rest were in bad shape. They began to surrender, at first in small groups and later in larger bands under white flags. In March 1864, 2,400 Navajos began the "Long Walk" to Fort Sumner. By the end of April 3,500 more made the march. Eventually, over 8,500 Navajos were held prisoner at Fort Sumner. Although a considerable number of Navajos went into hiding in the more remote canyon and mountain country to the north, south, and west, including some who found refuge with the Coyotero and other Western Apache bands, the Navajos had, in effect, been conquered.

The forty-mile-square treeless plain surrounding Fort Sumner was originally thought of as a place where the Navajos, along with the Mescaleros, were to be taught how to read and write, how to build villages, how to farm, and how to become "civilized" citizens. This plan sounded good on paper. But it was doomed to failure from the start.

Neither the Navajos nor the Mescalero Apaches were happy about being next-door neighbors. The Mescaleros had taken over the best farm land along the river, but they were moved off to make room for the more numerous Navajos. This didn't improve already hostile relations. As far as the Mescaleros were concerned, there were 9,000 Navajos too many in the area. They were right for the wrong reason, as the reservation was too small for even a tenth that many Indians. Bad water, bad food, lack of clothing and blankets, and disease took their toll of lives. Supplies promised by the government often failed to appear. If they did, they were poor in both quality and quantity. Plans for schools and farming instruction never materialized. Every year crops were planted and every year something happened—borers, worms, hail, frost, floods, drought. Bands of Comanches from the nearby plains raided the already small Navajo horse herds.

By November 1865, the Mescaleros had had enough of Fort Sumner. Overnight every Mescalero who could walk simply vanished. Only the sick and crippled were left, and within a few days they also disappeared. So did hundreds of Navajos, most of whom made their way back to their old homeland to join those renegade bands who had escaped capture.

Victorio, chief of the Warm Springs Apaches after the murder of Mangas Coloradas.

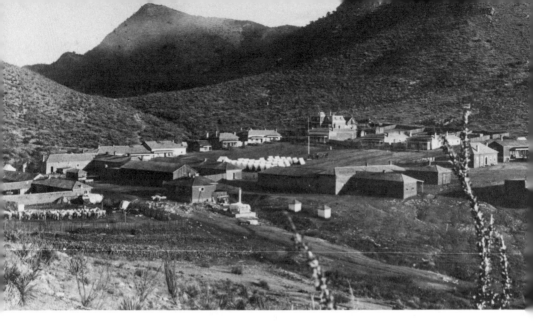

Fort Bowie, located at Apache Pass in the Chiricahua Mountains of southeastern Arizona, as it looked in 1886.

Affairs muddled along for another two or three years, with the Indian Bureau quarreling with the army's inhumane Indian policy. Finally, when American settlers began to complain about the good land the Navajos were occupying along the Pecos River, and federal officials were complaining about the tax money necessary to feed these thousands of prisoners, a treaty was signed at Fort Sumner on June 1, 1868. The treaty, signed by 29 Navajos headmen, allowed the Navajos to return to a new reservation in their former homeland in northwestern New Mexico and northeastern Arizona upon their promise to remain at peace. The federal government also agreed to buy sheep and goats to enable the Navajos to rebuild their pastoral economy. Within a few days long lines of ragged, underfed men, women, and children were slowly moving westward, and by the end of July more than 7,000 Navajos were back in their own home country.

Meanwhile, Cochise, Victorio, who had become the leader of the Warm Springs Apaches after the murder of Mangas Coloradas, and other leaders of the Chiricahuas and Western Apaches continued their raids against Mexicans and Americans. There were a lot more Americans to raid now that the big war back East was over. More gold had been discovered, and more people had flocked in, founding new towns at Prescott, Florence, and Phoenix in Arizona and along the Rio Grande in New Mexico. More forts and military camps were established: Lowell at Tucson, Bowie in Apache Pass, Whipple and Verde near Prescott, Crittenden on the Sonoita, Grant on the San Pedro, Goodwin near the Gila River, McDowell near Phoenix, Cummings and Bayard in southwestern New Mexico, McRae and Seldon on the Rio Grande. But still the army couldn't control the Apaches.

According to John P. Clum, one of the better Indian agents in the 1870s, the United States spent some 38 million dollars from 1862 to 1871 in its wars to exterminate the Apaches. During that period they killed less than 100 Apaches, including old men, women, and children, at the cost of the lives of more than 1,000 soldiers and civilians.

Unfortunately, most of the new settlers and soldiers, as well as many of the old ones, couldn't tell a friendly Indian from a renegade outlaw. They just couldn't realize that there were both good Indians and bad Indians. To them, all were savages, to be killed or imprisoned. To most Arizona pioneers every hostile Indian was an Apache.

Both in fiction and nonfiction, one reads of hundreds of raids and lootings and murders in Arizona in the 1860s and 1870s, from Prescott and Phoenix westward to the Colorado River, all credited to the account of the wild Apaches. But it just wasn't so. In the first place, that was not Apache territory. Although an occasional Western Apache hunting party might venture into the area, its chief inhabitants were the several bands of the Yavapai Indians. That had probably been Yavapai country for at least 900 years. These Indians were, and still are, usually miscalled Mohave-Apaches or Yuma-Apaches or Yavapai-Apaches. With the exception of those Western Apaches, particularly the neighboring Tonto Apaches, who married Yavapais, these Indians were not Apaches at all. They spoke an entirely different language, and their looks and customs were also different.

No doubt they did their share of raiding and looting, but practically all of their fighting was against other Indians along the

Colorado and Gila Rivers. Not until the 1860s did the Yavapais come into close contact with Americans. The Indians soon regretted this, as the newcomers, thinking the Yavapais were Apaches, immediately began to exterminate their red neighbors. The Yavapais naturally fought back. Between 1864 and 1876, however, an estimated 400–600 Yavapais were killed, many of them perhaps having been mistaken for Apaches.

Rarely was a white person ever punished for killing an Indian. Yet the slightest mistake by an Apache was immediately seized upon and heralded far and wide as another frightful Apache atrocity. News about Apaches had a habit of growing as it traveled. One or two Apaches might get drunk and kill a white man, perhaps the very same trader who had sold them the whiskey. By the second or third telling, the number of Apache raiders had increased to half a dozen. By the time the tale reached the nearest army post, the Apaches would number fifteen or twenty, with one of the famous Apache chiefs in command, and their innocent victims would have increased to five or six.

The infamous Camp Grant massacre occurred in 1871. A large group of Western Apaches under their chief, Eskiminzin, had camped a few miles from the army post for protection. So far as is known the Apaches were living in peace, cutting wild hay and selling it to the post. This was too much for certain citizens of Tucson. They wanted the Apaches exterminated, not pampered. Early one April morning an armed force of about 100 Mexicans and Papago Indians led by half a dozen Americans fell on the sleeping Indian camp and completely demolished it, killing some 100 Apaches, mainly old men, women, and children, and carrying off 28 youngsters to be kept or sold as slaves. Many of the Apaches, including Eskiminzin and his youngest child, managed to slip through the encircling line of attackers and reach the security of the hills. Eskiminzin's two wives and his five other children weren't so lucky, falling before the clubs and bullets and knives of the raiders.

When the news of the massacre finally broke, a wave of indignation swept the East. Eastern newspapers demanded an investigation of the bloody slaughter. But most western newspapers, from Denver to San Francisco, heartily applauded the raid, terming it a victory for peace. In justification for the raid local newspapers reported recent Indian raids near Tucson and along the San Pedro River, raids in which several Americans were killed and small herds of cattle and horses were stolen. These raids were made, so it was said, by Apache warriors from Eskiminzin's camp.

Eventually the ringleaders of the raiders were brought to trial in Tucson, but they were speedily acquitted. The jury was out only nineteen minutes. What was wrong, asked Arizona, with killing Apaches?

The Final
Apache Roundup

 THERE was a new day dawning for the Apaches of southern Arizona and New Mexico. To some of them the new day was good; to others it meant disaster. To the north, the Navajos had finally been put on a reservation of their own. So had the Jicarillas, although the location of their reservation was still changing every few years. Now it was the turn of the southern Apaches —the Mescaleros, Chiricahuas, Mimbres, Warm Springs, Mogollon, and Western Apaches—to learn firsthand the benefits and hazards of reservation life.

In 1871 the War Department brought in General George Crook, an able and extremely intelligent Indian fighter, to tame and round up all Apaches in Arizona except the Chiricahuas. Crook immediately began learning all he could about the Apaches and their country. He reorganized the army pack trains so that small units could move quickly to meet any emergency. On the advice of the Arizona governor, he hired fifty Mexicans as scouts but soon fired them when they proved to be incompetent, lazy, terrified at the very word Apache. In their place, over the violent objections of most Arizona citizens, he organized a company of Apache Indian scouts, paying them regular wages and putting experienced white

General George Crook and White Mountain Apache chief Alchesay.
ARIZONA HISTORICAL SOCIETY

scouts in command. Crook firmly believed that only an Apache could find another Apache, and time would prove him right.

But before General Crook could get his campaign going, President Ulysses S. Grant sent Vincent Colyer, the secretary of the Board of Indian Commissioners, West to attempt to place the Chiricahuas and other Apaches on reservations. Crook was forced to suspend operations, even though he was convinced that the Apaches had to be conquered before they would settle down peacefully on reservations. That set the pattern for the next few years. The Apaches became the central figures in a bitter tug of war between the United States army and the Department of the

Interior as to who was going to control the Indians and how the job was to be done.

In the two or three months Colyer spent in New Mexico and Arizona, he established reservations at Canada Alamosa in New Mexico for the Mogollon and Mimbres or Warm Springs Apaches, at Camp Apache, a new post set up in 1870 in Arizona's White Mountains, and Camp Grant for Western Apaches, and at Camp Verde and Camp McDowell for Mohave-Apaches (Yavapai Indians). He proposed a Chiricahua reservation on the Tularosa River in western New Mexico, but Cochise didn't like it. Colyer didn't visit the Mescaleros, saying that these Apaches had been at peace for some time and authorizing a reservation for them near Fort Stanton. Although several thousand Apaches, plus Yavapais, moved onto these reservations to receive rations, many others didn't.

Colyer had barely left Arizona before hostile Indians, including Cochise and his Chiricahuas, began to attack stages, freight caravans, and ranches throughout the territory. These events put the war party back in control in Washington. General Crook was ordered to punish all Apache bands not on reservations, and the distribution of rations to those Apaches on reservations was to be supervised by army personnel. Crook gave the Apaches time to return to the reservations by setting the deadline for their return for the middle of February 1872.

Again before Crook could begin his offensive, President Grant sent General Otis Howard to Arizona on another peace mission. About all Howard accomplished was to set aside a new San Carlos Reservation for Western Apaches north of the Gila River and adjoining the White Mountain Reservation. He took ten Apache leaders back East with him to see the sights of Washington and New York. But the Chiricahuas and other Apaches and Yavapais continued raiding, and Howard headed West again to negotiate a treaty with Cochise. Through the assistance of Tom Jeffords, a white friend of Cochise's, he was able to get the treaty signed and the Chiricahuas established on a reservation in the Chiricahua Mountains in southeastern Arizona. Most of the Southern Chiricahuas, under their leader, Juh, soon came up from Mexico and joined them. But there were still hundreds of hostile Apaches, including a great many Yavapais and neighboring Tonto Apaches, still on the loose.

Late in 1872 General Crook finally got his carefully planned military campaign under way. From his headquarters at Fort Whipple, near Prescott, he sent nine columns of troops into the field, each with its quota of Indian scouts. Aimed primarily at the Indians along the western edge of Apacheria, within a few months Crook and his scouts and troops had killed or rounded up most of the hostile Yavapais and Tonto Apaches and had shown the rest of the Western Apaches as well as the Chiricahuas that he meant business. Crook's Apache scouts stood the test of battle. Some Apache scouts even won the Congressional Medal of Honor for bravery.

For a few years there was an uneasy peace in Apacheria. General Crook wanted to make the Indians self-supporting through farming and stock raising so that they could sell their surplus food, hay, and cattle to the army. Many of the Apaches did begin to plant bigger crops. But Crook was bucking both politics and big business. The contractors in Tucson and other towns wanted to supply both the army and the Indians. They didn't want any competition from the Indians.

Apache scouts serving with the U.S. Army about 1883. ARIZONA HISTORICAL SOCIETY

Even with most of the Apaches now settled on reservations, conditions were not greatly improved from the point of view of the Indians. Dollar-hungry contractors and sticky-fingered Indian agents swindled the Apaches at the drop of a hat. Wagon loads of supplies that should have gone to the Indians wound up being sold to mining camps. Other agents doctored scales to make them weigh heavy, while crooked contractors added sand to flour and rocks to sacks of sugar supplied to Indian agencies. Corrupt whiskey peddlers preyed upon the Indian's weakness for liquor.

Indian agents came and went. Some were good; some were bad. Each had his own ideas about how to handle Indians. Even the best of them had little knowledge of Indians and Indian behavior. About the time they began to learn, they usually left.

There was no such thing as a consistent Indian policy. One day the Apaches would be treated as prisoners of war, the next as friends. If there was any one policy Washington had, it was to herd three or four thousand Apaches on a reservation, order them to be good, and put them on starvation rations. The Apaches bitterly resented these orders. They thought that as long as they remained at peace, they were keeping their part of the bargain.

It is impossible to detail all of the broken promises and agreements made by the whites with the Indians. In view of the treatment the Apaches received, it is amazing that so few actually rebelled and left the reservations.

At first, separate reservations were set aside for the different Apache groups. That worked for a time. However, with Cochise's death in 1874 some of the Southern Chiricahuas on the reservation began raiding across the border in Mexico. Cochise's two sons, Taza, who later died on a trip to Washington, and Nachez, seemingly lacked their father's strength of leadership. In late 1874 there were 830 Apaches reported on the Chiricahua reservation in southeastern Arizona. Of these, 275 were Mimbres or Warm Springs and Mogollon Apaches, 265 were Chiricahuas of Cochise's band, and 290 were Southern Chiricahuas from Mexico.

Then Washington decided that a concentration policy would be better, for it would put all the Apaches and associated tribes in southern Arizona and New Mexico on the San Carlos reservation. The government began this policy in 1875 by transferring 1,500

Nachez, the younger son of the noted Chiricahua chief, Cochise, and his wife.
SMITHSONIAN INSTITUTION, BUREAU OF AMERICAN ETHNOLOGY

Yavapais, including some Tonto Apaches, from the Verde reservation to San Carlos. Later in that year the San Carlos agent, John P. Clum, moved some 1,800 Western Apaches, mainly White Mountain Apaches, from Fort Apache to San Carlos.

In 1876, in an endeavor to put an end to raiding and other troubles, including the killing of a trader, the government ordered Clum to close down the Chiricahua reservation and move the Indians to San Carlos. But Clum could only round up 325 Apaches, mainly Chiricahuas under Taza. As many more lit out for Mexico when they heard the news, while 140 others wandered back to their old reservation at Warm Springs in western New Mexico. Finally, in May 1877, the 453 Apaches at Warm Springs were forcibly removed to the already crowded San Carlos reservation.

None of the Indians were pleased with this new concentration policy. The Western Apaches didn't want to share their reservation with the Yavapais or even with their close relatives, the Chiricahuas and Warm Springs Apaches. No one wanted to be integrated. Each group wanted a reservation of its own.

For the next nine years the Chiricahuas and Warm Springs and some of the other Apaches were in and out of the reservation. When they felt they were being mistreated or discriminated against, they left. When they began to run short of ammunition or when winter drew near, they rode back in and surrendered, to receive food, new blankets, and the freedom of the reservation.

If you read about 100-odd Apaches breaking out of the reservation and going on a raid, it sounds like a formidable force. But usually only about one-fourth of that number was the warriors. The others were women and children and elderly men.

It was a rare occurrence when several hundred Apache warriors got together at any one time. Navajos sometimes did, but only because they were a fairly large tribe. It probably happened only once or twice with the much smaller Chiricahuas and Warm Springs and Western Apaches. At the battle of Apache Pass in 1862 the combined Apache forces of Cochise and Mangas Coloradas have been estimated as high as 600 or 700. This is certainly far too high. Probably a figure somewhere between 300 and 400 warriors would be more nearly correct for the Apache Pass battle.

Most Apache depredations, in fact, were the work of small parties, from a dozen or two up to fifty or sixty warriors. Yet with such small numbers and often accompanied by women and children, the Apaches defeated forces that were vastly superior—better equipped, better armed, better fed.

Old Nana's raid in the summer of 1881 is typical. After Victorio and many of his mixed band of Warm Springs and Mescalero Apaches had been killed at Tres Castillos in Mexico in 1880, Nana had taken charge of the survivors. Nana was in his 70s at the time, half-blind and badly crippled with rheumatism. Yet this old man led 15 Warm Springs Apaches and some 25 Mescaleros on a raid from Mexico throughout southwestern New Mexico. In approximately 6 weeks he and his band covered over 1,000 miles of desert country while closely pursued by over 1,000 soldiers and civilians, fought 10 or 12 battles and won them all, killed an estimated 40 or 50 soldiers, miners, and ranchers, and wounded 100 others, stole several hundred horses and mules, and finally escaped back to Mexico with the loss of only a few men.

In the summer of 1881 a White Mountain Apache medicine man began inciting the Apaches by telling them that when the white men left, their dead chief would return to lead them to prosperity. In August of that year, when soldiers from Fort Apache went to Cibecue to take the medicine man prisoner, the Indians, including half a dozen Apache scouts, rebelled and killed a number of soldiers and one officer. But the medicine man was also shot and killed, and, lacking a strong leader, the Apaches soon surrendered.

Hundreds of troops were immediately rushed into Arizona to insure against further uprisings. The presence of so many soldiers on the reservation made the already suspicious Indians even more edgy. In September, thinking that the soldiers were going to round them up because of the Cibecue outbreak, Juh and Nachez led seventy-odd Chiricahuas off the reservation. Raiding, looting, and killing, they cut a bloody path across the border into Mexico.

In March 1882, three of the Apache scouts who had rebelled at Cibecue were tried and hanged at Camp Grant, and two others were sent to Alcatraz. This, most Arizonans thought, would end the trouble. But it only marked the beginning of four long and bloody years of warfare.

Nana, chief of the Warm Springs Apaches after the death of Victorio.

Loco and some 700 Warm Springs Apaches, including many Chiricahuas, had remained on the reservation when Nachez and Juh left for Mexico. Loco was getting along in years and could see no future in war with the White Eyes. But Nachez and Juh thought differently. They needed Loco and his large following to reinforce their numbers. They also needed Loco's influence, as he was now one of the most respected Apache leaders, even if they had to use force to get it.

In April 1882 Nachez and Chato and some 50 Chiricahua and Warm Springs Apaches slipped across the border and made their way unseen through the patrolling soldiers to Loco's camp. Possibly persuaded at gunpoint, Loco reluctantly agreed to leave. Almost the entire band of 700 including, of course, many hundreds more women, children, and old men than warriors, headed south. Within ten miles of the post they looted a wagon train, and within a week they had killed some 50 ranchers and teamsters and stolen many horses and mules. After a couple of engagements with the United States army, which the Indians won, they crossed into Mexico. There they were ambushed by the Mexican army and suffered their heaviest casualties. Most of the 70-odd Indians killed were women and children who had been at the head of the fleeing column.

With most of the Warm Springs and Chiricahua Apaches now on the loose, the citizens of Arizona and New Mexico were again in an uproar, expecting an attack at any moment. General Crook, who had left Arizona in 1875, was recalled to the territory to restore law and order on the reservations. But before he got there, trouble broke out once again among the Western Apaches. Some fifty Cibecue Apaches, still resentful over the killing of their medicine man the previous year, swept down on San Carlos. Ambushing and killing the white chief of the agency police and three of his Indian policemen, they took off for the Tonto Basin, pillaging ranches, stealing horses, and wounding or killing those who got in their way. But the hostiles were soon overtaken by the army, and most of them were either killed or captured.

Crook arrived in September 1882 and immediately began touring southern Arizona, talking to Indians, agency officials, and army officers. Within a short time he got rid of crooked agents and unauthorized squatters on the reservations, allowed the White Mountain Apaches to return to their own high country near Fort Apache, put trusted officers in charge at San Carlos and Fort Apache, and encouraged the Indians to raise more crops and cut more hay and firewood which they could sell to the army.

For a few months there was peace in Arizona. But Crook knew that sooner or later some of the hostile Chiricahua and Warm Springs Apaches now in Mexico would begin raiding north of the border. He also knew that the only way to capture the Apaches was to trail them across the border to their strongholds in the Sierra Madre Mountains of Mexico. Grudgingly, the Mexican government gave permission for Crook to cross the border in pursuit of hostile Indians. Crook began preparing by bringing in trainloads of necessary supplies, the railroad having been completed across southern Arizona and New Mexico in 1881. But above all Crook began hiring and training more and more Apache scouts.

Finally, in March 1883, came the long awaited outbreak. Chato, Chihuahua, and Bonito led a small band of twenty-four Warm Springs and Chiricahuas across the border into Arizona. Rivaling old Nana's raid for daring, in six days they rode some 400 miles, stealing fresh horses whenever they needed them. Plundering and murdering, they fought their way across southeastern Arizona and southwestern New Mexico and back into Mexico. They killed at least 25 Americans and Mexicans and lost only 2, one killed in Arizona and the other willingly surrendered to the army. This turned out to be an extremely important capture. For the Indian, Peaches, claimed that he was a White Mountain Apache married to a Chiricahua woman and that he had been taken off the reservation against his will. He had left the hostiles because his close friend had been killed and he had had enough of raiding. Now he was ready to guide Crook into the Sierra Madres.

This was the break Crook had been hoping for. With Peaches as guide, he set out for Mexico on April 23, 1883. He left most of his troops behind to guard the border, taking with him only a handful of officers, a small company of 42 men, and nearly 200 Apache scouts. More than 200 miles south of the border Crook sent Captain Emmett Crawford and Lieutenant Charles Gatewood deeper into the Sierras with 40 or 50 of the Apache scouts to track down the

Peaches, a White Mountain Apache scout who guided General Crook's party into the Sierra Madres after Geronimo.

hostiles. Surprising Bonito's camp while most of the men were away raiding Mexican settlements, they killed several men and captured a number of women and children. Through these Indian captives, Crook established contact with the camps of the hostiles, telling them he would wait for three days for any communication from the Apaches.

Within less than twenty-four hours the Indians began coming in to General Crook's camp, first women and children, then later, one by one, the leaders of the various bands—old Nana, Loco, Bonito, Chihuahua, Geronimo, Nachez. Most of them told Crook that they were tired of the constant fighting and running. They were, more than anything else, stunned by the fact that American troops, led by scouts of their own blood, were confronting them in their supposedly impregnable stronghold in the Sierra Madres. Now all they wanted was peace and the chance to return to the reservation.

Geronimo proved to be the hardest to convince. He wanted preferential treatment. But Crook bluntly told him his choice was peace or war: to go back to the reservation or stay in Mexico and be hunted down. Crook's gamble paid off: Geronimo gave up. But he hedged by saying that he needed time to round up the rest of his and Nachez's followers, who were widely scattered in the mountains. Crook couldn't wait. His supplies were low, and he had been in Mexico completely out of touch with what was going on in Arizona Territory for too long a time already. Normally he wouldn't have trusted Geronimo under any circumstances, but now he could only hope for the best. He gave Geronimo permission to round up the rest of the hostiles and come in as quickly as possible. Geronimo assured Crook that he would be in in two moons (four weeks).

Crook immediately set out for San Carlos, arriving there on June 23 with 325 Chiricahua and Warm Springs Apaches—273 women and children and 52 men, including Nana, Loco, and Bonito. Nachez, Chato, Mangas, Geronimo, and nearly 200 others remained in Mexico, supposedly to find other hostile Indians still in the mountains. Crook sent Lieutenant Britton Davis and a company of Apache scouts to wait at the border and escort the Indians to the reservation when they crossed. Davis had a long wait: the moons came and went and still no sign of the hostiles.

The local and even the national newspapers had a field day: they wanted to know who had captured whom. General Crook, they said, came back with the women and children while the other Apaches continued raiding and killing in Sonora and Chihuahua. The newspapers and the vast majority of the territorial citizens were against the policy of amnesty for the renegades. Nobody believed that the rest of the Chiricahuas and Warm Springs would keep their word and surrender peacefully.

Arizona and New Mexico war contractors, of course, wanted the uprising to continue because they were making handsome profits from supplying the army with everything from hay to horses. If hostile Indians ran off 100 head of army horses, the contractors could always supply more, at a profit, naturally.

Lieutenant Davis and his scouts continued to wait at the border. The weeks continued to pass without a sign of the hostiles. Then, early in 1884, Nachez and Zele and a dozen or so warriors and twice that many women and children rode into Davis's camp and were escorted to San Carlos. Davis went back to the border to wait some more. On February 27 Chato and Mangas and fifty or sixty more Apaches showed up at the border and were taken to San Carlos. Finally, on March 14, 1884, some eighteen moons after the date he had originally set, Geronimo and fifteen or sixteen men and some 70 women and children rode up to Davis and his scouts, driving ahead of them a huge herd of cattle stolen south of the border.

But the Apaches didn't get to enjoy their stolen stock. Once the Indians were back on the reservation, the cattle were taken from them and sold, and the proceeds turned over to the Mexican government for distribution to their original owners. Geronimo and his followers bitterly resented this, as they claimed they had been promised protection for both themselves and their horses and cattle.

In May 1884 the Chiricahua and Warm Springs Apaches, now reduced in number to 512, were moved to Turkey Creek, some fifteen miles south of Fort Apache. This was higher and more wooded country and suited the Indians better than the lower, treeless flats around San Carlos. Crawford and Davis proposed giving them sheep and cattle, but the Indian Bureau said they had to become farmers. Some of them took to it, but many were not happy. Perhaps if the attempt had been made to turn them into herdsmen rather than farmers, the experiment might have been successful.

Peace had come once again to southern Arizona and New Mexico, but it was an uneasy peace. There was no trouble with the Western Apaches, for over the years they had become accustomed to reservation life. Farming was not strange to them as it was to many of the Chiricahua and Warms Springs Indians. Most of the Western Apaches had been raising crops of corn, beans, and squash for nearly 200 years. Moreover, they were still in their original homeland. They were not displaced persons like the Chiricahua and Warm Springs Apaches.

In addition, there was considerable dissension among the Warm Springs and Chiricahua Apaches themselves. Ill-feeling between Chato and Geronimo split these Indians into two groups, two-thirds or more favoring Chato, the balance, largely through the influence of Nachez and Chihuahua, favoring Geronimo.

Geronimo was probably the most famous individual in Apache history. Few people remember such names as Mangas Coloradas, Victorio, Juh, Loco, Nana, Chato, Santana, Diablo, or Nachez. Even the name Cochise is not as well known as that of Geronimo. Yet Cochise, Mangas Coloradas, Victorio, and many other Apache leaders were greater warriors and chiefs than Geronimo and were so rated by their own people.

Geronimo's father had been the son of a Southern Chiricahua or Nedni Apache chief living in the Sierra Madres of Mexico. He married a woman of one of the southwestern New Mexico Apache groups, possibly a Mogollon Apache. In accordance with Apache custom, he was required to leave his own family and move to his wife's homeland. By so doing, he relinquished his right to succeed his father as chief of the Nednis. According to most authorities, Geronimo was born in eastern Arizona along the Gila River where Clifton, Arizona, now stands. His Apache name was Goyokla (One Who Yawns). Mexicans gave him the name by which he became known to late-nineteenth-century Arizona and New Mexico settlers and troopers, Geronimo (Spanish for Jerome), supposedly applied because of his bravery in fights in Mexico.

So far as we know, Geronimo was neither a chief nor a subchief. In 1880 during a census taken on the Apache reservation, the names

Geronimo, perhaps the best known of all Apache war leaders.

of the chiefs of each group were recorded. Geronimo's name does not appear on this list. By showing skill and daring as a fighter and by utilizing his knowledge as a shaman, or medicine man, Geronimo became the leader of a small group of renegade warriors. A number of Chiricahuas, however, have denied that Geronimo was a medicine man, any more so than any other average Chiricahua, each of whom felt he or she had some kind of "power."

After Juh's death, Geronimo claimed the leadership of the Southern Chiricahuas, but the following was confined to less than thirty men. In the words of half a dozen army officers and civilian agents who knew him, he was feared and disliked by a majority of the Chiricahuas. Many who went along with him did so only through fear.

Geronimo was a man of words as well as action. He seems to have been an excellent speaker. As one man who knew him said, Geronimo would rather talk than eat, and he loved his food.

It may well have been this feature that brought Geronimo into prominence during the summer of 1883. Up until that time Geronimo was relatively unknown in comparison with Juh, Victorio, Nachez, Nana, Loco, and other Apache leaders. According to some authorities, General Crook thought that he could reach the hostile Apache chiefs through Geronimo because of Geronimo's ability as a speaker. Geronimo's reputation was made, and he quickly became a national figure. Many of the subsequent raids made by Nana, Nachez, and Chihuahua were credited to Geronimo. It was an easy mistake to make in those days of relatively primitive communications. From then on no single Apache name was more widely known and feared than that of Geronimo.

By the spring of 1885, two other factors added more fuel to the flame of discontent sweeping the Chiricahua and Warm Springs Apaches. These were the prohibition against the making and drinking of tiswin (tulapai), a drink made from fermented corn, and the prohibition against mistreating wives, particularly against cutting off the end of the nose of unfaithful wives. The Indian men were incensed at this interference with their personal affairs. With Nana, Geronimo, Chihuahua, and Nachez stirring them up, they became more and more unruly.

Lieutenant Davis was aware that a dangerous situation was developing and sent such a message by telegraph to General Crook. But the message was never delivered. Within a few days it was too late.

On May 17, 1885, after an attempt on Lieutenant Davis's life failed, 144 Chiricahua and Warm Springs Apaches jumped the reservation and headed for Mexico. Of this number 35 were men, 8 were boys of fighting age, and 101 were women and children, with Geronimo, Nachez, Nana, Mangas, and Chihuahua leading them. Chato and Loco and Zele managed to keep the other three-fourths of the Chiricahuas and Warm Springs on the reservation.

According to information Davis received later, Geronimo would not have had so many with him if he had not told the Indians that Lieutenant Davis had been killed and that they would all be hanged for his murder. When Mangas learned the truth, he and his small group split off and never rejoined the others. Chihuahua and his large party also left and tried to slip back to the reservation. But they were spotted by Apache scouts hot on their trail and decided to strike out on their own. While Geronimo and Nachez fled to safety in the Sierra Madres, Chihuahua and his band crossed into New Mexico and swept southward. Raiding ranches for horses and ammunition and killing at least twenty people, they finally escaped across the international border, but not before killing five soldiers and looting three wagon loads of government supplies.

General Crook sent two columns of troops and Apache scouts into Mexico on the trail of the Indians. In a move designed to prevent the hostiles from sneaking back across the line to raid and loot, he placed guards at every water hole and mountain pass along the border, with mounted patrols on the move day and night. But Crook well knew that no numbers of troops could seal the border permanently against the slippery Apaches.

So did southern Arizona and New Mexico citizens. Ranches were barricaded or deserted as their owners fled to the safety of the nearest town. Farmers tilled their fields with rifles slung from their plow handles.

Over the next seven or eight months about all the troops did was chase the renegades back and forth across the border. The campaign cost the lives of two officers and eight soldiers, seventy-three American civilians, twelve reservation Indians, and an untold number of Mexicans. The Apaches lost just six men, two boys, two women, and one child, most of whom were killed by Apache scouts, not by regular army troops. In addition the scouts captured a number of Apache women and children. The Apache scouts, in fact, including Chato and many other Chiricahua and Warm Springs Apaches, were primarily responsible for the eventual subjugation of their fellow Indians.

Finally, late in 1885, Crook realized that these tactics weren't getting him anyplace. He sent a select battalion of Indian scouts —Chiricahuas and Warm Springs and Western Apaches—across the border on the trail of the hostiles. His strategy paid off. In January 1886, after Crawford's tragic death at the hands of Mexican troops, the Apache scouts contacted the renegades. Geronimo promised to meet General Crook near the border in two moons. Nana and eight other Indians accompanied the scouts back to the border.

On March 25, 1886, considerably more than two moons later, Crook met with Geronimo, Nachez, Chihuahua, and Nana. After two days of talks Geronimo and the others agreed to surrender on the condition that they would be sent East as prisoners, along with their families, for a period not to exceed two years. Crook prepared to leave the next morning for Fort Bowie. But that night a whiskey peddler sneaked into the Chiricahua camp and began selling liquor to the Indians. By the following morning Geronimo, Nachez, some sixteen warriors, and about a dozen of the younger women had taken off for the mountains.

Nana and Chihuahua and the remaining eighty Apaches kept their word and turned over their weapons to Crook, who immediately shipped them all off to Florida by train. But Crook was criticized so severely because he had let Geronimo and his small band of Apaches slip out of his grasp that he resigned his command.

General Nelson A. Miles, the noted Indian fighter, was brought in to take charge of running down Geronimo. Miles took no chances. He asked for more troops and began hiring 300 more Apache scouts. He also introduced the heliograph, or signaling mirror, into the Southwest. Using this portable device, an operator could flash messages in Morse code by reflected sunlight across fifty miles of desert from one station to another. The

Apaches knew about "talking wires," as they called the telegraph, and they knew how to stop them by cutting out a length of wire. But this new system of flashing lights completely mystified them.

Even before General Miles could get fully organized in his new job, Geronimo and Nachez and a dozen other Apaches crossed the border into southern Arizona, raiding and killing down the Santa Cruz valley. Some of them even got as far north as the Apache reservation before they finally turned back toward Mexico. Then began one of the most intensive manhunts in history. Some 5,000 troops and nearly 500 Apache scouts chased the handful of hostile Chiricahuas. Hundreds of Mexican troops were also in the field. But none of them ever caught up with the Indians.

Like his predecessors, Miles had to learn that mounted cavalry couldn't run down Apaches, not, at least, in this southwestern desert and mountain country. According to the cavalry manual, the United States cavalry could and did ride forty miles a day under emergency conditions. The Apaches, however, rode seventy miles a day and even more if hard pressed.

Miles switched his tactics. He dismissed most of the Indian scouts, keeping only a few for use as trackers. To replace Crook's scout columns, he organized a cavalry command along with some infantry under Captain H. W. Lawton and Leonard Wood to operate south of the border. A few days in the Sierras finished the horses, and the cavalry joined the infantry on the ground. But they still couldn't catch up with the hostiles. Finally, learning that the Apaches had been talking to Sonora Mexicans about possible surrender, Miles returned to Crook's policy and sent Lieutenant Gatewood and two Chiricahua scouts to contact Geronimo. In a little more than a month Gatewood reached the hostile camp, where the two scouts delivered Miles's message that, upon surrender, the Apaches and their families would be sent to Florida. After considerable discussion, Geronimo and Nachez agreed to go north to meet with General Miles.

Nobody captured Geronimo and Nachez and the other hostiles; they gave themselves up. They rode north to their conference with Miles still carrying their rifles and other arms, escorted by Gatewood and Lawton and their small troop of scouts and soldiers primarily as protection against possible attacks by Mexican soldiers.

Mangas, son of Mangas Coloradas, and one of the Warm Springs Apache leaders.
SMITHSONIAN INSTITUTION, BUREAU OF AMERICAN ETHNOLOGY

On September 3, 1886, Miles finally arrived at the camp in Skeleton Canyon, and after extended talks Geronimo and Nachez accepted the surrender terms. By September 8, Geronimo and Nachez and their followers were on a heavily guarded train headed for Florida. With them, also as prisoners of war, went the two Chiricahua Apache scouts who had located their camp and had helped persuade them to surrender.

They were not the only Apache scouts to be so rewarded for their services to the government. General Miles had been giving considerable thought to the nearly 400 Chiricahua and Warm Springs Apaches still on the reservation at Fort Apache. Though these Indians had remained peaceful throughout the latest uprisings, nearly all of the men having served as scouts under both Crook and Miles, Miles believed them to be a possible source of danger and acted accordingly. At about the same time that Geronimo was getting on the prison train in southern Arizona, Miles's troops rounded up all the Chiricahua and Warm Springs Apaches at Fort Apache and put them on trains for Florida.

But the Apache wars were not yet over. When the Apaches had left the reservation in May 1885, Mangas and his small band of two men, three women, and six youngsters had split off from the others and had gone deep into the Mexican Sierras. There they had remained until early in October 1886, when they decided to return to the reservation. On their way north they picked up fifty-odd mules from a ranch in Chihuahua. This ranch, however, happened to be managed by ex-Lieutenant Britton Davis, who had resigned from the army the previous year. Davis and his ranch hands followed the Indians' trail until he determined where they were heading and then telegraphed the information to General Miles. Captain Charles Cooper, with twenty soldiers and two Fort Apache scouts soon found the Indians, and Mangas and his party surrendered without resistance. This was, as Davis has recorded, the only actual capture of armed Apache warriors during the entire campaign. Davis eventually got his mules back and Mangas and his followers were sent to Florida to join their fellow tribesmen in prison.

The Apache wars had finally ended without a shot having been fired. But the government's broken promises and treachery continued to haunt the Chiricahua and Warm Springs Apaches. The hostiles had surrendered with the understanding that they would be united with their families in Florida. But the women and children were held at Fort Marion, while Geronimo and his warriors were kept under guard at Fort Pickens, several hundred miles away.

Nor was Florida quite the paradise that had been painted for Geronimo and the other Apaches. The close confinement and the humid climate proved to be too much for many of these free desert dwellers. Five hundred and two Chiricahua and Warm Springs Apaches had been sent to Florida. Within a year their numbers had been reduced to 447.

Protests by prominent citizens finally aroused interest in the case. Dozens of solutions were proposed but none was workable. One proposal suggested the Indians be sent back to their native home, but Arizona's citizens raised such a storm of protest that it was quickly dropped. The controversy did produce one result. Late in 1887 all the Apaches were transferred to Mount Vernon Barracks, Alabama. They were just getting used to this when they received orders to move to Fort Sill, Oklahoma. This action brought another storm of protest, now from New Mexico. That state's citizens said the Apaches would be within 500 miles of their former homeland, and that, argued the citizens, was much too close for comfort.

In spite of this, in the fall of 1894 the 407 Indians still alive were moved to the military reservation at Fort Sill. The Apaches were pleased with the move. Here they were back in open country more like their desert country than anything they had seen since. They were able to build houses of their own and to farm small patches of land. Nachez and Chato and a number of the others even became government scouts.

But a promised allotment of land never materialized, and in 1911 there was an attempt to take away what little land they did have. This was too much for the Apaches. They got together and asked for a place where they could live without constant fear of removal. For once their plea was heard. In October 1911 the government sent a delegation of Chiricahua and Warm Springs Apaches back to New Mexico to look over several possible sites for a permanent home.

The Apaches had hoped to return to their former Warm Springs reservation in western New Mexico. But one look changed their minds. The country wasn't the same as they remembered it. Overgrazing and erosion had all but ruined the pleasant little valley. After considerable discussion and dissension, they finally decided on the Mescalero Apache reservation east of the Rio Grande. Not all the Apaches wanted to go. Many of the Warm Springs band had made homes for themselves in Oklahoma and elected to stay. When the time came to move in April 1913, only 187 Apaches, mostly Chiricahuas, boarded the boxcars for New Mexico. There they have remained with their Mescalero and Lipan cousins, not quite home but close enough to smell the warm desert wind and taste the desert dust.

Of all the Chiricahua and Warm Springs Apache chiefs who led their fighting warriors during the 1880s, only one, named Dutchy, met a violent death, being killed in Alabama in 1891. Loco and Nana died of old age soon after they reached Fort Sill, and Chihuahua also died at Fort Sill of tuberculosis. Geronimo lasted until February 1909, while Nachez and Chato spent their declining years on the Mescalero reservation. All of the great Chiricahua and Warm Springs Apache chiefs are now gone, but many of their children and grandchildren are still living on the Mescalero reservation or in and around Apache, Oklahoma.

The Chiricahua and Warm Springs Apaches, including all Gila Apaches—Mimbres, Warm Springs, Copper Mine, Mogollon, or whatever they were called—suffered more trouble and hardship than any other Apache groups. Living as they did in southern Arizona and New Mexico next to the international boundary, they were exposed to attacks from both Americans and Mexicans. The quarter of a century from 1861 to 1886 was, with the exception of a few short years of peace, one of continual warfare between the Chiricahua and Warm Springs Apaches and the United States and Mexican armies. Heavily outnumbered but never outfought, these Apaches were reduced from an estimated 1,500 to less than one-third that number. In addition, the entire tribe was made prisoners of war and taken away from their homeland.

Most of the other Apache tribes weren't, however, much better off at the close of the Apache wars. Most of them also lost heavily in numbers, particularly the Lipan. The few Lipan on the Mescalero reservation were joined by a small group from Mexico in 1905. Most of them still lived in at least a part of their original homelands, yet they were subject to the whims of Indian agents. The army still maintained its posts at Fort Apache, San Carlos, and Fort Stanton, and other forts still stood guard duty around the edges of the reservations. Greedy white men were still chipping away at the Apache lands. With the end of the Apache wars one chapter in Apache history came to a close and another opened.

7

The Apache
Way of Life

WHEN the Apaches left Canada and migrated southward, they were all nomadic hunters and seed gatherers, moving with the seasonal flow of animal and plant life. By the time most of them reached the Southwest, they had picked up farming from some of the sedentary Plains Indians living along the Missouri River or its major tributaries from Montana to Kansas. Once in the Southwest they gained still more farming skills from the Pueblo Indians and from the incoming Spanish and Mexican settlers.

The Kiowa-Apache may, in fact, have been the only Apache tribe that did no farming at all until the modern era. Like other nomadic Plains Indians, the Kiowa-Apache lived primarily upon the buffalo, as did the Lipan, who also had small gardens of corn, beans, and squash. But with the coming of the horse and the Comanches in the eighteenth century, most Lipan Apaches were forced to abandon their fields and return entirely to hunting and gathering and raiding.

Farming was not of any great importance to the seventeenth- and eighteenth-century Mescalero, Chiricahua, and Gila Apaches (Mimbres, Warm Springs, Copper Mine, and Mogollon). The

White Mountain Apaches drying squashes and multicolored Indian corn during harvest time.

WESTERN WAYS PHOTO BY CHARLES W. HERBERT

only real Apache farmers were the Jicarilla Apaches, the Navajos, and the Western Apaches. All of them raised the three native Indian staples—corn, beans, and squash. Corn came in a variety of colors—white, yellow, red, blue, black, and speckled. Beans also came in different colors—pink, black, white, yellow, and spotted. The amount of farming varied from group to group. In some, the majority of people farmed or had access to farms or farm products. In others, only a few farmed. Chiefs or rich men usually hired others to work their fields, paying them in farm produce.

Both dry farming and irrigation were practiced. Not having

much running water in their country, Navajos generally dry farmed, planting the seeds deep to draw on underground moisture. Western Apaches often irrigated their fields by damming small streams and digging ditches to carry water to downstream fields. There might be from five to a dozen or more farms strung out along one ditch. Ditch bosses were important individuals in Western Apache farming, supervising the repair of dams, the cleaning out of ditches, and the distribution of water to the farms.

Fields were never very large. Both men and women prepared and planted the fields, but weeding was more often done by women, as was harvesting.

The mainstay, however, of most Apache diets was wild plant foods—seeds, nuts, fruits, roots, and berries. Wild plants made up a third of the yearly food intake of farmers and well over half of that of nonfarmers. The variations in terrain within Apache territory, from low, dry deserts to high, forested mountains, supplied them with a great variety of wild plants. Almost everything that grew was useable, and a great deal of it was edible. In fact, the Indians found something equivalent to most of our fruits, vegetables, sweets, and flavoring materials.

Perhaps the most important wild plant foods were acorns, pinyon

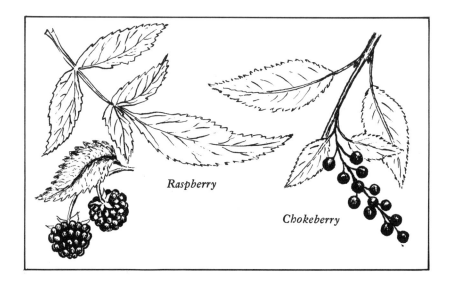

Raspberry

Chokeberry

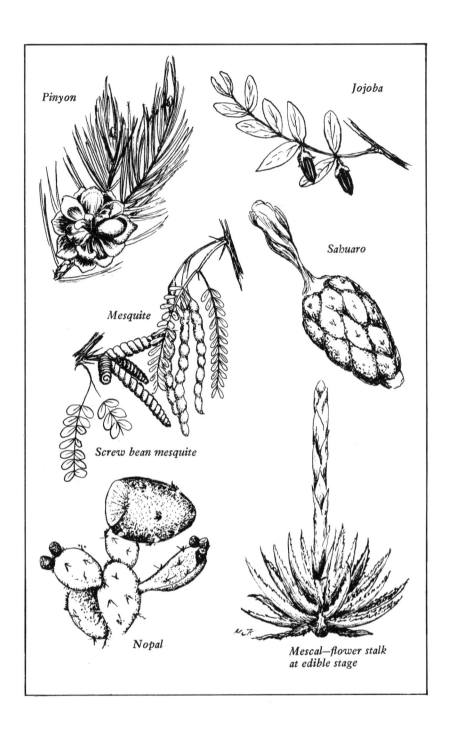

Pinyon

Jojoba

Sahuaro

Mesquite

Screw bean mesquite

Nopal

Mescal—flower stalk
at edible stage

nuts, agave or mescal heads, mesquite beans, and juniper berries. But the Apaches also gathered several kinds of wild onions and wild potatoes, wild mountain celery, sumac berries, cattail roots, wild plums, hackberries, maroposa lily bulbs, the fruit of nearly every kind of cactus from prickly pear to giant sahuaro, yucca fruit, wild walnuts, leafy greens such as wild rhubarb, pigweed, beeweed, and milkweed, currants, mulberries, chokecherries, and locust flowers. Tiny seeds are the specialty of a dry country, and Apache women gathered their share to be made into flour or mush —pigweed, goosefoot, sunflower, Indian millet, mountain grass, tumbleweed, and several varieties of mustard. Most Apaches made tea from various herbs such as mistletoe and marigold. Gum chewing is an old Indian custom, and Navajos and other Apaches made gum from the Colorado rubber plant and from the root of orange sneezeweed.

Several varieties of tobacco were gathered wild, and the Navajo and some other Apache tribes even planted small patches of it, perhaps borrowing the idea from the neighboring Pueblo Indians. Tobacco and tobacco smoking played an important role in almost every public ritual or ceremony. Tobacco was, however, relatively scarce before the coming of white traders, and the social smoking of cornhusk cigarettes was considered a great luxury.

The importance of the growing seasons of wild food plants may be seen in the Chiricahua Apache division of the year into six time periods:

LITTLE EAGLES—early spring
MANY LEAVES—late spring and early summer
LARGE LEAVES—midsummer
LARGE FRUIT *or* THICK WITH FRUIT—harvest time of late summer
                                          and early fall
EARTH IS REDDISH BROWN—late fall
GHOST FACE—winter time

The Chiricahua Apaches called the entire year "one harvest" and reckoned time in terms of harvests rather than years.

The gathering of wild plant foods was women's work and was usually done communally. If food was to be gathered near home, two or three might go together. For a longer trip, a larger group of women would get together. For a journey of more than one day, men would go along to protect the women.

Hunting and gathering wild plant foods kept the average Apache family almost constantly on the move during much of the year. The first wild plant crop appeared in the early spring with the sprouting of the yucca or Spanish bayonet and the agave or century plant or, as it is commonly called, the mescal. Generally this meant a journey to the places where these plants grew most abundantly.

Both plants had to be cooked before they could be eaten or stored. Young shoots or stalks of the mescal plant could be roasted over open fire and peeled and eaten like sugar cane. But most Apaches, like other southwestern Indians, usually cooked mescal in large quantities, drying and storing the surplus. To do this, they cut the entire head or crown out of the center of the plant with a sharp stone or iron blade set in a wooden handle or with an equally sharp chisel-shaped stick. Then they had to dig a cooking pit big enough to hold a ton or so of the mescal heads. If an old pit was handy, the women cleaned it out; if not, they dug a new one ten to twenty feet in diameter and from three to five feet deep. After lining the hole with rocks, they filled it with wood, covered the wood with more large rocks, and set it afire. When the fire burned down, the mescal heads were piled on top of the hot rocks and covered with wet grass, brush, and dirt to keep in the steam and heat. The mescal heads were left to bake in this steamy fireless

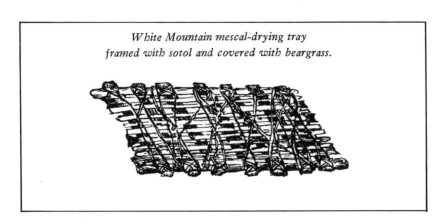

White Mountain mescal-drying tray
framed with sotol and covered with beargrass.

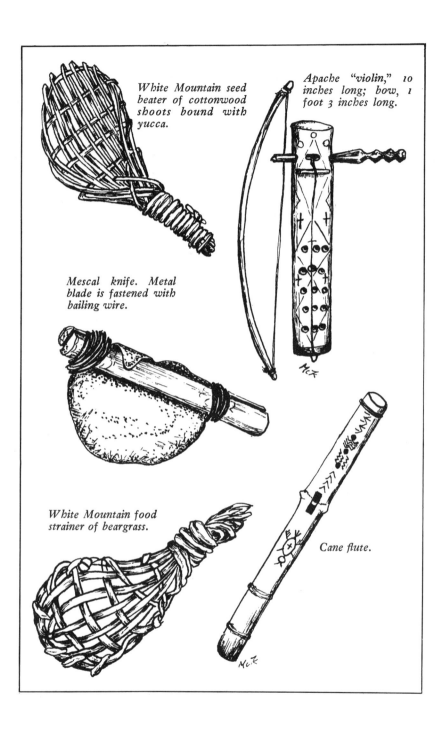

White Mountain seed beater of cottonwood shoots bound with yucca.

Apache "violin," 10 inches long; bow, 1 foot 3 inches long.

Mescal knife. Metal blade is fastened with bailing wire.

White Mountain food strainer of beargrass.

Cane flute.

cooker for a day or two until they were thoroughly baked. The mescal could then be eaten as it was or cut up and dried and stored for future use. Sometimes families had to make several trips before they had enough mescal stored away for winter. Such dried mescal would keep almost indefinitely.

Mescal was a favorite food of most Apache groups, particularly the Mescaleros, who were so named by the Spaniards because of their taste for mescal.

Yucca fruit was another staple food which was stored in quantities for winter use. The fruit was cut up, sun-dried on stones, ground up and made into cakes, and then roasted before being stored.

In May farming Apaches returned to their home fields to clean and repair ditches and prepare the fields for planting. Farm-owning families usually stayed until the first part of July, when the corn was up six or eight inches. Then most of the families left, leaving a few old people and children to take care of the growing crops.

Most Apaches moved to the lower country to pick the ripening prickly pear and sahuaro cactus fruit. By the latter part of July most of them were gathering the first of the seed-bearing plants, greens, sumac berries, and such wild fruits as raspberries, strawberries, grapes, and currants. About the same time came one of the most important of the wild food harvests—the acorns from several varieties of oak trees. This harvest might last a month or more. After this it was time to pick mesquite beans.

By September farming families began drifting back to their farms where crops were ripening. After harvesting, most of the corn, beans, and squash were dried and stored away in underground caches. Lined with smooth, flat stones, their tops covered with rocks and tightly plastered with mud, these pits safely protected the baskets and skin sacks of food from the elements and hid them from the eyes of outsiders. Many of the wild plant foods were also dried and stored in similar caches for use during the lean winter months.

By the time the harvest was completed and stored, pinyon nuts and juniper berries were ripening and had to be gathered. Late fall was also a favorite time for deer hunting.

While women were harvesting wild foods, men spent most of

White Mountain Apache woman brushing the spines off prickly pear cactus fruits before gathering them in her handwoven basket.

their time hunting, their primary occupation. By the age of seven or eight most Apache and Navajo boys were bringing home small birds, prairie dogs, squirrels, or rabbits which they had shot with bows and arrows.

Although hunters occasionally went out alone, most hunting was done in organized groups. Hunters were armed not only with bows and arrows but also with offerings and prayers, as hunting was usually accompanied by ceremony and ritual.

The deer was the most important big game animal for most Apaches. Eastern Apaches, of course, hunted buffalo whenever they could. Other game animals included antelope, elk, mountain sheep, cottontail rabbits, and wood rats. Most Apaches wouldn't eat or use fish or snakes or frogs. Even today, most of them maintain strong taboos against eating or touching anything that lives in or around water, which probably stem from ancient religious beliefs. Most Apaches were quite superstitious, regarding certain birds and animals, such as bats, bears, and snakes, as bad omens. They hunted badger, beaver, and otter for their fur and killed or trapped birds such as the eagle for their feathers.

The raid was for centuries a recognized part of Apache economy. They were after loot, not glory. The cattle, mules, and horses garnered in these raids furnished a considerable portion of the Apache meat supply. Without it many would have starved. The Apaches did not consider such raids stealing. They believed that, given the same chance, the Mexicans would do the same to them.

The Navajos began raiding the New Mexican ranches and Pueblo Indian villages at an early date. While they probably ate the first sheep and goats they stole, eventually they began raising them on their own. These animals then formed a major part of their economy.

This was not the case with the southern Apaches. Although Mescaleros, Gila Apaches, Chiricahuas, and Western Apaches raided Spanish and Mexican settlements for over 200 years, they never seriously attempted to raise stock of their own. Perhaps this was because horses and cattle were too easy to acquire by raiding. Actually, many Apaches didn't particularly need horses in prereservation days. They moved in a relatively restricted area, farming and gathering and hunting. One of the few times horses

Navajo woman shearing one of her flock of sheep near Gallup, New Mexico.

TAD NICHOLS

came in handy was on a raid, and then they could easily be stolen.

Like their Ice Age predecessors of 10,000 B.C., the Apaches preferred to eat horses rather than ride them. Given the choice, they would take mule, burro, and horse meat over that of cattle, sheep, or goats. Navajos were the exception, preferring goats and sheep to mules and burros. To the average Apache a horse was a fast and handy means of getting from place to place. If the horse then dropped dead from exhaustion, it served as roast for the moment and as jerky (meat dried in the sun) for the future, while the long intestine made an excellent canteen. Then the Apache would start hunting for another horse to steal.

From the last of November until early spring, hunting was almost the only economic pursuit. Winter was a favorite time for visiting relatives in other localities. Families frequently traveled to one of several main camping areas in the lower country to escape the winter weather in the mountains. From these camps raiding or war parties would penetrate into Mexico. Women would catch up on their mending and other long-neglected household chores, and men would repair their old weapons and make new ones. Winter was a time for storytelling and relaxing after the strenuous round of activities of the spring, summer, and fall.

8

Wickiups
and
Baskets

THE division of labor was fairly simple among most Apaches, men and women having their own spheres in the daily round of activities. Apache men are still careful not to be seen doing anything considered strictly women's work, as others, both men and women, may ridicule them. Men will cook or build a temporary house only when there are no women around to do it.

The men took care of the meat supply, raided, fought in feuds or in war, looked after such stock (horses, mules, and cattle) as they might have, made their own tools and weapons, and helped with such heavy work as had to be done. As fighting men, most Apaches felt it was beneath them to engage in much physical labor. To take care of their weapons and, of course, use them when necessary was about all that society could and did expect of them.

The men, therefore, left it to the women to take care of everything else. The women cooked, cared for the children, built and maintained the houses, carried in the water and firewood, made the household implements and utensils, tanned hides, made the clothing, gathered whatever wild plant foods were in season, and did most of what farming was done.

Navajo old-style, six-sided hogan built of squared logs. TAD NICHOLS

As one old White Mountain Apache grandfather once told this writer, "When the men were at home, they sat around and smoked and told stories." Then, with a twinkle in his dark eyes, he added, "At the same time they might also repair any of their weapons or tools that might need fixing."

Not all Apaches lived in the same kind of houses. Some, like the Navajo, lived in earth-covered lodges, called hogans, while the Lipan and Kiowa-Apache used the buffalo hide tipi of the plains. But most Apaches preferred to live in circular, dome-shaped brush dwellings called wickiups. This was the favorite home of the Western Apache, Chiricahua, Mescalero, and Jicarilla. These were not makeshift huts crudely thrown together in a few hours. A good wickiup might take the women two or three days to build.

In its simplest form a wickiup was made by setting long willow or oak poles in shallow holes around a rough circle, bending over the tops, and tying them together with yucca leaf strands. Over this conical or dome-shaped framework the women house builders then tied bundles of bear grass or similar thatching material, shingle style, with yucca strings. A smoke hole opened in the top above a central fireplace. In wintertime or in rainy weather the wickiup was covered with skins to make it watertight. Later, when canvas could be obtained through trade with whites, this was commonly used to rainproof the wickiups. A low entrance hole was left, customarily facing to the east among many Apache tribes, as this was the favored sacred direction. A heavy hide was suspended on a cross-beam over the entrance so that it could be swung either inward or outward.

Wickiups ranged from eight to fifteen feet in diameter and stood seven feet high at the center. Entirely covered with skins or canvas, these wickiups were warm and comfortable in the coldest weather.

Western Apaches thatching a wickiup with bundles of bear grass.
WESTERN WAYS PHOTO BY CHARLES W. HERBERT

In summer the skins could be rolled up around the bottom and the thatch taken off to catch the cooling breeze.

Nor were these wickiups dirty just because all of them had floors of hard-packed dirt, as good a floor as you could have found at that time among any of the southwestern Indian tribes. In fact, the standard house floor the world over, except for houses raised on poles, was, and still generally is, the ground itself. Floors were swept with a stiff grass broom or a leafy branch.

Living as the Lipan and Kiowa-Apache did among the Plains Indians, these two Apache tribes naturally adopted the Plains Indian dwelling—the portable, skin-covered tipi. Again it was the women's job to put the tipis together. Lashing together with rawhide the small ends of three or four smooth, twenty-foot long poles, several feet from the top, they raised these and spread the legs to the desired diameter, generally from ten to twenty feet. Over these they laid ten to twenty similar poles, interlocking their tips with those of the already tied poles. Over this framework they stretched the buffalo-hide cover made of ten to fifteen dressed buffalo hides carefully tailored and sewn together in one piece. This cover was pinned together in front with long wooden pins, leaving a low doorway at the bottom, which usually faced toward the east. This doorway was covered with a stiff buffalo hide weighted at the bottom to form a self-closing door. In warm weather the cover could be rolled up from the bottom to allow ventilation, while in winter the outer edge was either staked to the ground or anchored with heavy stones and banked with earth.

To regulate the smoke rising from the central fireplace and to prevent the wind from blowing smoke back down into the tipi the Plains Indians developed a smoke vent. Sewn to the cover at the sides of the smoke hole in the top of the tipi were two earlike skin flaps, each tied to a long pole. By shifting these poles the smoke vent could be operated like a chimney, opened wide in good weather or practically closed in stormy weather.

Through contact with the Plains Indians in buffalo-hunting days, both Mescalero and Jicarilla Apaches took over the buffalo-hide tipi as an alternate home. But in their mountain homelands the wickiup seems to have been the more favored of the two.

Erecting one of these tipis sounds like a long and difficult job, but

Lone Wolf's Kiowa camp about 1870. Kiowa-Apaches lived in similar camps with the Kiowas in the high plains country during the eighteenth and nineteenth centuries.

actually it wasn't. A couple of women could put one up or take it down in no more than half an hour. But moving a tipi from one camp to another wasn't quite that easy. For one thing, the buffalo-skin cover of the average tipi weighed 100 pounds or more. For another, the two-dozen odd lodgepoles had to be carted along also, as suitable poles weren't always available on the treeless plains.

To solve this transportation problem some imaginative Plains Indians invented the travois. They strapped a V-shaped frame of poles to their dogs, with a rawhide netting midway toward the dragging butt ends of the two poles to hold the load in place. Since a strong dog could only drag a load of fifty to seventy-five pounds, tipi covers had to be made in two pieces and carried on

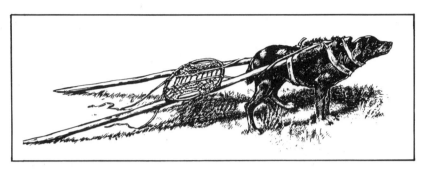

Plains Indian dog travois.
SMITHSONIAN INSTITUTION, BUREAU OF AMERICAN ETHNOLOGY

two travois. The rest of the lodge poles had to be dragged in the same way. Half a dozen miles was a good day's journey for a band of Indians moving camp in this manner. After the introduction of horses, however, they switched the travois to the new animal and were able to cover much more ground.

Most Navajo hogans blend so well into their desert and rocky mesa background that you can drive past one only 100 yards away and never notice it. Navajos were not quite as nomadic as most of their fellow Southern Athabascans and usually lived in more permanent houses.

Their earliest houses that archeologists have found were circular forked-stick hogans, with three upright forked juniper poles forming a conical foundation for other poles and bark and a final heavy coating of mud and dirt. A low covered doorway usually projected slightly toward the east. Later, they built circular hogans of slabs of sandstone with cribbed log roofs covered with earth. Still later, they began building six- or eight-sided hogans of horizontally laid logs, the upper tiers gradually drawing in toward the center to form a dome-shaped roof which was covered with hard-packed earth. They also built circular hogans of upright logs and square or rectangular ones of stone, all with slightly domed, earth-covered roofs. These hogans were all windowless, the only entrances or exits being the doorway facing in an easterly direction and a smokehole in the center of the roof.

Unlike most other Southern Athabascans, Navajos did not live in

Rectangular Navajo hogan built of stone in western New Mexico.

camps or even small villages. Following their sheep and goats in search of greener pastures, they moved with the seasons, each family generally having two or three hogans in widely separated areas. Near almost every Navajo hogan were several other structures— a brush or stone corral; a flat-topped, brush-covered ramada, or shelter used as an outdoor cooking or work area; and a ceremonial or purifying sweat lodge, a miniature copy of the old mud-coated, forked-stick hogan.

During cold or rainy weather all cooking and sleeping was done inside the wickiup or tipi or hogan. Lining the walls were brush and grass beds over which skins or robes were laid. These were used not only as beds but also as chairs. In warmer weather people spent the greater part of their time, both awake and asleep, outside under a ramada. These ramadas were built of four large corner posts connected with cross-beams and poles and roofed with willow or bear grass thatching. There were no side walls.

Household equipment among most Apache families was not very abundant. Because the Apaches lived a nomadic life, their implements and utensils had to be light and portable. These included several different kinds of baskets, an occasional clay pot, gourd cups and plates and spoons, all sizes of skin bags, bone and wooden awls, stone metates and manos (grinding tools), a digging stick or two, and wooden fire drills.

If the Apache Indians specialized in any of the arts and crafts, it was basketry. So far as we know, the Kiowa-Apache made no baskets, and we don't know anything about Lipan basketry. But all other Apache peoples made baskets in abundance. Baskets are a necessity for seed-gathering peoples—for collecting, for winnowing (sifting), for storage. Moreover, baskets are light and portable.

Like seed gathering, all basket making was done by the women. Apache women were excellent basket makers. They constructed them by several different methods in at least four different varieties —bowls, storage jars, burden or carrying baskets, and pitch-covered water jars.

Basketry trays or bowls were the most common variety of baskets. Bowls with sides flaring up and out at angles ranged from two to ten inches in depth and from four to thirty inches in

Burden Basket	*Western Apache Storage Basket*	*Western Apache Coiled Bask*

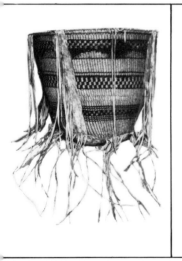  

*White Mountain Apache basket maker twining a burden basket. The water baskets
on the right are newly made, those on the left covered with pinyon pitch to make
them watertight.*

WESTERN WAYS PHOTO BY CHARLES W. HERBERT

diameter. They were used for almost everything around the household—winnowing seeds or grain, holding meal, parching corn,
boiling food, serving as platters for stews, mashing berries, and
holding water. Tall baskets with flaring sides tapering in to a
small neck with a high rim were used for the storage of dry
materials.

Bowls and storage jars were constructed by a process called
coiling. Three peeled willow or cottonwood twigs formed a tri-
angular, ropelike foundation which was coiled up spirally, beginning at the center of the basket at the bottom. Each coil was
sewn to the next by a thin willow or cottonwood splint inserted
through holes punched in the foundation by a sharp bone awl.

Most Apache basket makers decorated their bowls and storage
jars with simple black geometric designs which contrasted with the
light cream or tan color of the willow and cottonwood splints.

To make black designs the basket makers used the dark outer covering of the seed pod of the wild devil's claw plant. Like all Indian basket makers, the Apache women wove the basketry designs following a plan carried only in their minds.

These basket makers also made large carrying or burden baskets in a twined weave, usually of split sumac twigs, sometimes of willow. These large, broad-mouthed baskets were decorated with three or four horizontal colored bands encircling the basket and also with hanging fringes of narrow strips of buckskin and, in more recent times, with dangling tin cones or pendants.

Apache water jars or canteens were actually twined-woven, pitch-covered baskets. In a land where water was often scarce, canteens were highly important household items. These narrow-necked jars were tightly woven of split sumac twigs, with a hide handle often woven into each side. To make them watertight, the

Burden baskets and cradleboards at the White Mountain Apache Fair at Whiteriver.
WESTERN WAYS PHOTO BY CHARLES W. HERBERT

inside, and frequently the outside as well, was coated with melted pinyon pitch. A piece of yucca with the fibrous end shredded or a stick with a buckskin rag tied to it was used to paint the melted pitch on the jars. Sometimes red ocher, one of the fairly common iron minerals found in natural deposits, was rubbed over the outer surface before the pitch was applied. This served not only to fill in the tiny crevices between the stitches but also to form a decorative effect, as the red showed through the pitch when the latter dried and hardened. Both small and large water jars were made, the larger ones frequently being made to hold tiswin. When water was carried in one of these canteens, the top was plugged with a wad of clean grass or juniper bark.

Basket making may sound simple and easy, but it wasn't. The Apache basket maker had to know a lot about materials and techniques. She had to know where and when to gather the best materials. Sewing splints had to be given a uniform size by scraping. Then they were tied in coiled bundles and stored for future use. The devil's claw pods had to be gathered in the fall when they were dry, split, and tied in bundles for storage.

While most Apache baskets were much alike, the basketry of each tribe was distinct from that of the others. Western Apache baskets were usually black and tan in color, with small coils and fine even stitches. Chiricahua basket makers often used yucca leaves as sewing materials, giving a soft green, sometimes brown, tone. So did Mescalero basket makers. But the Mescaleros weren't as good craftswomen. The coils of their baskets were thin and loose, and their stitching was often coarse and irregular. The Jicarilla, as we have mentioned, were so named because of their small basketry drinking cups. They were expert basket makers, using sumac twigs for both sewing splints and foundation rods, the latter often five in number rather than the usual three. Their basketry was distinguished by its heavy, wide coils, by loop handles on bowls, and by the shiny brown background of the sumac.

So far as we know, all Southern Athabascans except for the Lipan and Kiowa-Apache formerly made pottery. This is unusual, as most nomadic peoples can't be bothered with lugging around heavy pots and pans which can be broken so easily. Moreover, Southern Athabascan pottery is unique in the area. We aren't exactly sure when and where and from whom the Southern Athabascans learned the art. We don't think they picked it up on their long migration south from Canada. The only parallels to it are some twelfth- and thirteenth-century prehistoric Pueblo pottery dug up in northern New Mexico and historic Ute and Southern Paiute pottery found in southern Colorado, Utah, and Nevada.

Southern Athabascan pottery was characterized by its dark gray or black color, a pointed or conical base, and flaring rims with raised or incised decoration. Tall, relatively narrow cooking vessels were the most common shapes found. Such pottery was made fairly commonly by the Navajo, slightly less often by the Jicarilla, even less frequently by the Western Apache, and only to a limited extent by Chiricahua and Mescalero Apaches. The Navajos were the only ones who made decorated pottery similar to that of the neighboring Pueblo Indians, from whom they probably acquired the art. They decorated jars, bowls, and canteens with brown or black designs on a cream or light tan background.

Pottery making, like basketry, was women's work. To begin a vessel, a lump of the right kind of clay was molded over the knee to form the conical base. To this base, coils of clay were added to build up the side walls. After drying it was baked hard in a hot fire.

Of all the items of Apache household furniture, the heaviest and bulkiest were the implements used to grind up seeds and corn and other dry foods. These grinding or milling tools were the metate and mano. The metate (an Aztec Indian term) was a flat, rectangular slab or sandstone or lava on which corn or seeds were ground by crushing and rubbing back and forth with a smaller hand stone. Archeologists call the hand stone a mano, after the Spanish word for hand.

But not many Apache women made their own manos and metates because it was too hard work. First they had to find stones of the right kind and size and degree of hardness. Then these stones had to be slowly and carefully chipped into shape with another smaller stone. It was much easier to find metates and manos abandoned around the ruined villages of the former inhabitants of the region, the prehistoric Pueblo Indians. In the 1930s when a party of University of Arizona archeologists was uncovering

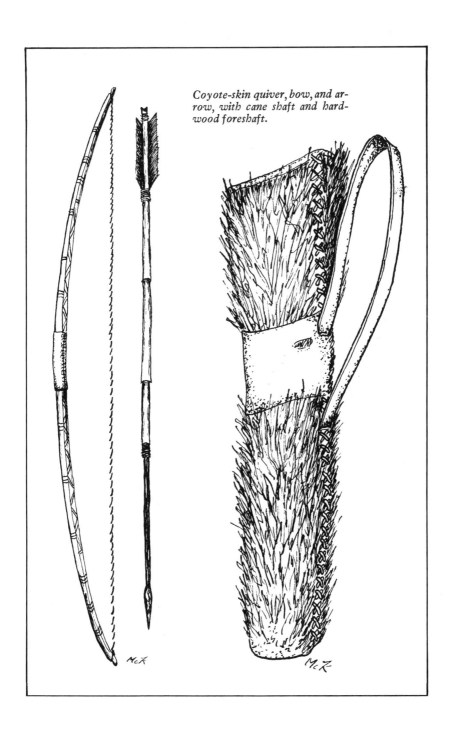

Coyote-skin quiver, bow, and arrow, with cane shaft and hardwood foreshaft.

Kinishba Pueblo, near Fort Apache, many Apache men and women came almost daily to watch our excavations. They were particularly interested in the hundreds of metates and manos we were constantly digging up in the ruins and quickly packed off all those we did not want.

Another job for Apache women was the tanning and preparation of hides. Most Southern Athabascans used more deer, antelope, and elk hides than anything else. However, the eastern tribes living next door to buffalo country—the Lipan, Kiowa-Apache, Mescalero, and Jicarilla—also used a great many buffalo hides. The hair was left on those skins to be used as blankets or robes and was scraped off all others with a sharpened deer bone or stone. To transform the stiff rawhide into soft buckskin, the women rubbed warm deer brains into the skins and stretched and worked them until they were soft and pliable.

In addition to clothing, the women made from these tanned skins bags and containers of all sizes, water carriers, cases for bone awls, knife sheaths, and pollen bags for their sacred meal. Skins were

Prehistoric Pueblo Indian trough-shaped metates excavated by the University of Arizona at Kinishba Pueblo near Fort Apache and eagerly grabbed by White Mountain Apaches to grind their corn.

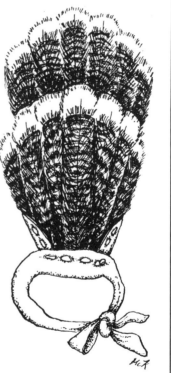

White Mountain turkey decoy set in buckskin base.

San Carlos cowhide double bags decorated with pierced leather over red flannel.

sewn together with deer sinew as thread and a bone awl from the sharpened leg bone of a deer to punch holes in the skins.

Many Apaches frequently dyed their tanned skins. They made dark brown dye from the juice of wild walnut hulls, red from the boiled root and bark of the mountain mahogany, and yellow from algerita roots or from yellow ocher.

Another common item of household equipment found in most wickiups was a baby carrier or cradleboard. A Western Apache baby normally had two carriers, a small temporary one made at the time of birth and a larger, permanent one made three or four months later.

The permanent cradleboard was made of a single piece of pliable ash, oak, or peeled mesquite root. This was bent into a long flat oval about forty inches long and twelve to fourteen inches wide, with the overlapping ends toed at the top. Across this, close-spaced slats of sotol stalks were lashed with rawhide thongs through holes burned in the ends of the slats. Near the top of this framework was fastened a hood or canopy made of thirty to forty horizontally placed peeled catclaw twigs. The open top of the hood was covered with buckskin painted with yellow ocher. To make the carrier comfortable a soft padding of shredded bark or crumpled grass was covered with a tanned skin of a fawn or cottontail rabbits, fur side up. The baby was laid on this and covered with a second tanned skin. The baby was then lashed into the carrier with a strip of buckskin passing from side to side through a series of buckskin loops on each side of the framework. The mother supported the cradleboard on her back by a buckskin carrying strap across her forehead.

Various small objects were usually attached to the hood, both to amuse the child and to serve as charms or amulets. These might include bags of pollen, tails of squirrels, pine cones, prehistoric shell beads, and stone arrowheads. A Chiricahua Apache mother generally hung the right paw of a badger, with grass substituted for the bone, on the cradle to guard the child against fright, for fright lies at the root of a number of serious illnesses. She often tied a length of cholla wood on the cradle to ward off colds and other sickness. Pieces of wildcat skin and hummingbird claws also served as cradleboard charms.

A young Navajo brave still in his cradleboard. TAD NICHOLS

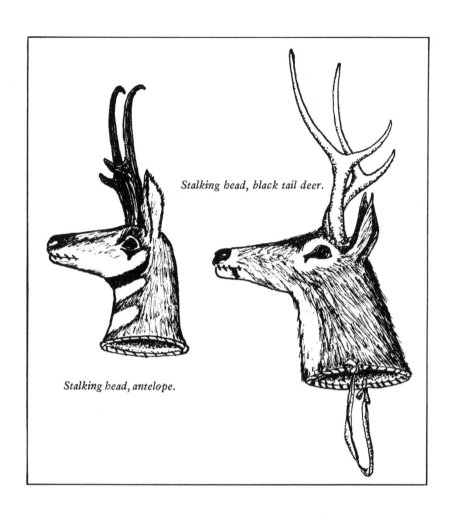

Stalking head, black tail deer.

Stalking head, antelope.

Although the fire was closely tied in with the household and women's work, it was the Apache man who made the fire drill and who used it most frequently. This Apache match consisted of a flat piece of sotol stalk or yucca and an eight-to-ten-inch pencillike stick of dry wood, juniper or sotol, together with dry juniper bark and dry grass. These two sticks were wrapped and carried in a skin bag tied to the belt or put in the quiver when the men were on a trip. Navajos often used split sections of willow or sagebrush as the fire hearth and a smooth hardwood twig for the drill.

To light a fire, the fire maker set one end of the pencillike stick in a small hole in the flat piece of sotol and twirled the stick rapidly back and forth between the palms of his hands. In a short time the fine wood powder formed from the friction heated up and dropped through a side notch in the hole onto the tinder, the dry grass or bark placed below. When the fire maker blew on the hot, smoking tinder, it broke into flame. That is, it flared up if the fire maker was an expert. If he was a beginner, it might have taken a great deal longer. Fire making was only one of the many things an Apache boy had to learn how to do.

After European contact, of course, flint and steel or flint and iron pyrites were also used to strike sparks and light a fire. To furnish light in the camp or to carry fire from one camp to another, strips of juniper bark were tied together to make a long torch. As late as the last half of the nineteenth century Lipan Apaches still preferred to light fires with the old-style fire drill. By rubbing the end of their dogwood twirling sticks in sand, they were able to make a fire more easily and quickly.

Hunting and raiding took up much of an Apache man's time. Still, in order to hunt and raid effectively, he had to spend a lot of his time at home repairing his old weapons or making new ones. Before the Apaches acquired guns from the Europeans, bows and arrows, spears and lances, clubs, and knives made up the Apache man's hunting and fighting equipment. Yet even after they acquired guns, a bow and arrow remained the warrior's most trusted weapon, one that never misfired and, if broken, could be quickly repaired or replaced.

Bows were usually made of wood from mulberry, oak, or locust trees. The average bow was three to four feet long with a single curve, although double-curved bows were occasionally made by the Chiricahuas. After the wood was cut, smoothed, and properly seasoned, it was bent, tied, and put in hot ashes. After it cooled, the bow retained its curved shape. When Chiricahuas made a double-curved bow, they bent the heated bow between two young trees growing close together. The outer surface of the bow was generally painted some solid color, with a few decorative designs or the maker's identification marks on the inside. Bowstrings were of split deer or bison sinew twisted together into a single cord.

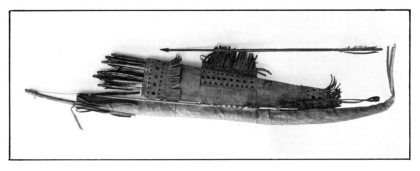

Chiricahua bow and arrows said to have been used by Geronimo.
HEARD MUSEUM OF ANTHROPOLOGY AND PRIMITIVE ART

The sinew-backed bow was made and used by the Navajo, Jicarilla, and probably Mescalero, Lipan, and Kiowa-Apache. This type of bow was backed along its length with strips of sinew. Chiricahuas sometimes wrapped a worn and weakened bow with sinew.

Most Southern Athabascan tribes—Navajo, Mescalero, Jicarilla, Kiowa-Apache, and probably Lipan—commonly used a wooden arrow, while the cane arrow with foreshaft was the favorite among the Chiricahua and Western Apache. The latter had a cane or reed shaft, into the end of which a hardened foreshaft was fitted. For their solid wooden arrows Chiricahuas used mulberry or mountain mahogany. Arrows were usually about thirty inches long and were often decorated with bands or strips of black, blue, or red paint. To the butt of the shaft three split tail or wing feathers from the eagle, red-tailed hawk, or buzzard were tied on with wet sinew or sometimes also with pinyon pitch.

Flint arrowheads were commonly used when they could be found around prehistoric Indian ruins. Yet there seems to have been little attempt by the Indians to make their own stone points. Iron was sometimes used for arrow points when it could be obtained. But generally the wooden tip of the hardwood shaft was simply seasoned and hardened by heating and charring with fire.

In the hands of a strong man an Apache bow made an effective and powerful weapon. An Apache could kill a deer at 100 yards and could shoot an arrow clear through a deer at 15 yards.

Navajo warrior and hunter with lance and shield in 1893.
SMITHSONIAN INSTITUTION, BUREAU OF AMERICAN ETHNOLOGY

Quivers and bow covers were frequently made of mountain lion skin, with the fur and tail left on. Deer, antelope, wildcat, and other skins, with the fur either left on or scraped off, were also used. The average Chiricahua warrior or hunter usually carried from thirty to forty arrows in his quiver. Rawhide wristguards protected against the impact of the bowstring.

Seven-foot-long spears or lances were made from sotol stalks or other woods, with the point fire hardened. After European contact spears were tipped with iron knives or bayonets to make a still more deadly weapon. Spear shafts were usually painted in one or more colors, and a couple of eagle tail feathers were tied to the shaft, sometimes near the point, sometimes near the butt end. Normally such spears were not thrown but were used by the Apache warrior only when he was on foot.

To make a war club a Chiricahua man covered a round, fist-sized stone with rawhide and tied it by a short piece of rawhide to the end of a wooden handle also often covered with buckskin. A loop of buckskin was attached to the handle for a hand hold. In addition, a horse's tail or, more recently, a cow's tail was often tied to the end of the handle.

Before the introduction of metal by the Europeans, Apaches made chipped stone knives. Both the Chiricahua and Western Apache often used rawhide slings to hurl stones when hunting birds and even deer.

Chiricahua, Western Apache and Navajo warriors used circular hide shields. Since these were made primarily of cowhide, they may have been a recent acquisition. Some had buckskin covers sewn over the rawhide, and most were painted with sun symbols, morning stars, or other designs. Eagle feathers were often attached to the outer edge of the shield. These shields seem to have been connected as much or more with ceremonialism as with actual defense.

Lipan Apaches, however, like most Plains Indians, carried large oval shields made of thick bull bison hides. Unless a hit was dead center, arrows and even rifle bullets usually glanced off such shields.

When the Apaches secured horses around the middle of the seventeenth century, they began making saddles and bridles and such other equipment as they could neither trade for nor steal. For saddles many Apaches used two rolls of rawhide stuffed with grass. Others made a saddle modeled after Spanish ones, with a cottonwood framework covered with rawhide. Long ropes were made of buckskin or rawhide, bridles of braided horsetail hair, and fringed quirts (riding whips) of braided rawhide. In the unlikely event an Apache didn't have any rawhide, he could make a serviceable rope by shredding yucca leaves and braiding the tough strands together.

The products of an individual's handiwork were, in theory, his own. Except for land and stores of food, property was individually owned. A house was occasionally spoken of as "ours," but it actually belonged to the woman who had built it, as did also the baskets and the other domestic articles she made. What she did with them other than operating her own household was her business.

What a man made, his weapons and his tools, were his own, and his wife could not get rid of them without his consent. On the other hand, a man could not give away all the plunder he had secured in a raid without being subject to criticism and ridicule both inside and outside his own family.

Long Hair
and
Moccasins

 APACHE men, women, and children all wore their hair long. Most of the eastern Apache men—Mescaleros, Jicarillas, Lipans, and Kiowa-Apaches—wore their hair in two braids, following the fashion set by their Plains Indian neighbors. Most eastern Apache women also wore their hair long and braided, although Lipan and Mescalero women sometimes had it done up in a queue.

Among the Chiricahua and Western Apaches, however, men wore their hair loose and unbraided. To keep it out of their eyes they tied a strip of buckskin, later a piece of flannel or other cloth, around the head. Like their husbands and brothers, Western Apache and Chiricahua women tended to wear the hair hanging loosely. Many younger women, however, along with some of the older ones, parted the hair in the middle, gathered it at the back, and wrapped it in a knot.

Apache men didn't wear mustaches and chin whiskers or beards, because most of them couldn't grow mustaches or beards even if they had wanted to. Like most members of the Mongoloid family of races, their facial hair was normally scanty. Another reason, particularly among the Chiricahua, was that facial hair was considered undesirable. The growth of any such hair was usually thought to indicate disobedience of some kind. Older Chiricahuas warned youngsters in training not to get water in their noses or mouths or they would grow mustaches. They also warned them not to smoke when they were small or they would get mustaches.

What little facial hair Apaches did have they plucked out with their fingernails or with shell tweezers. Later on, when true metal tweezers could be obtained either through trade or raid, every Apache man carried a pair as standard equipment. When a man couldn't buy or steal a pair of tweezers, he made his own by splitting the end of an empty metal cartridge case and flattening the split ends. During the 1930s I often saw older White Mountain Apache men whiling away an idle moment by plucking out stray whiskers with just such homemade cartridge case tweezers.

The Apache was proud of his heavy head of hair. Among the Mescaleros there were ceremonies for children which were intended to insure a good shock of hair.

When a Western Apache youngster was two or three years old, the hair was cropped close in the spring so that it would grow out long and thick. This practice was followed in the belief that everything starts fresh in the spring of the year. This spring cutting of children's hair—either cutting it off completely or merely bobbing it short—is still observed among some Apache groups.

Like most other southwestern Indians, Apaches manufactured hair shampoo from the root of the yucca plant. When this root was pounded and soaked in water, it made a lather that both looked and cleaned like soapsuds. After washing their hair, Apaches often rubbed in deer fat to make it lie flat and stick together.

Neither the Chiricahuas nor Western Apaches ordinarily wore feathers in their hair. The only ones who sometimes did were those Apaches living next to the Plains Indians—the Mescalero, Jicarilla, Kiowa-Apache, and Lipan. In later days these Indians often adopted the huge feathered headdresses so typical of many of the Plains Indians. A Western Apache or Chiricahua medicine man's round buckskin cap, something like a skullcap, might be decorated with eagle or raven feathers clipped off short. But that was the extent to which feathers were worn in the hair.

In the early days the Apaches, like most other southwestern

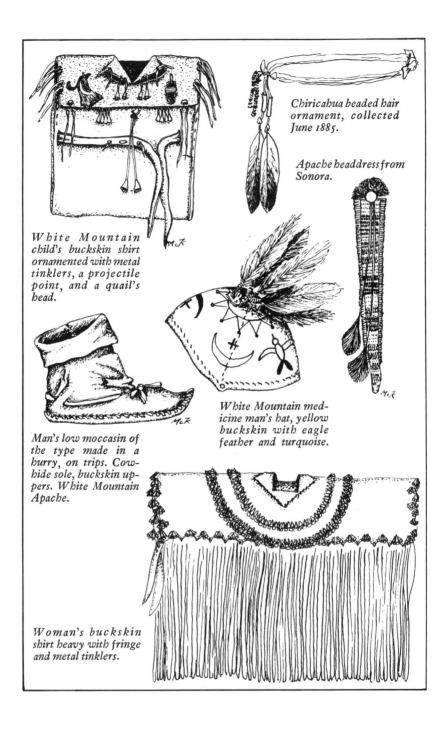

Chiricahua beaded hair ornament, collected June 1885.

Apache headdress from Sonora.

White Mountain child's buckskin shirt ornamented with metal tinklers, a projectile point, and a quail's head.

White Mountain medicine man's hat, yellow buckskin with eagle feather and turquoise.

Man's low moccasin of the type made in a hurry, on trips. Cowhide sole, buckskin uppers. White Mountain Apache.

Woman's buckskin shirt heavy with fringe and metal tinklers.

Indians, made their own clothing out of animal hides, usually deer-skin. The Pueblo Indians of northern Arizona and New Mexico, along with most of the Pima and Papago Indians in southern Arizona, were almost the only Indians in the United States to wear clothing made of home-grown and home-woven cotton cloth.

Traditionally the Apache men dressed in long-sleeved buckskin shirts, broad skin loincloths or breechcloths, and high moccasins. The breechcloth (sometimes called breechclout) consisted of a long strip of buckskin hung over a belt in front, with the long end drawn between the legs and tucked up under the belt in back. In warm weather most men wore only the breechcloth and, of course, moccasins.

Perhaps the most important part of the Apaches wearing apparel were the bootlike moccasins made of soft buckskin with rawhide soles. The hard sole generally extended well beyond the toes and turned upward in a distinctive tip. War moccasins had an even more distinctively shaped front, with the extended sole cut into a rising disk. The upper part of the moccasins was soft buckskin and could be pulled up to the knee or thigh or folded down. These folds formed handy pockets in which to carry knives or paints or other small objects.

When an Apache man was raiding or hunting or fighting, he wore a buckskin or rawhide belt with an attached knife sheath of buckskin. Although the Apache man's basic costume in former days consisted of buckskin shirt, breechcloth, and moccasins, these differed slightly from tribe to tribe.

Women's dress in early days also varied somewhat from tribe to tribe. Jicarilla and Kiowa-Apache women wore dresses of buckskin reaching from the shoulder to below the knees, with an extra buckskin cape or poncho over the head and shoulders in colder or rainy weather. Lipan, Mescalero, Chiricahua, and Western Apache women wore a two-piece dress of buckskin—a medium length skirt and a poncholike jumper or shirt. All, of course, wore bootlike moccasins with characteristic turned-up toes.

The Mescalero Apaches clung to the traditional Apache costume of buckskin shirt and breechcloth as long as they could. In fact, United States authorities weren't able to get Mescalero men into

Pair of Western Apache buckskin moccasins.

TAD NICHOLS

Changes in Apache men's and women's clothing styles. Prewar at left; war years in center; late 1880s and reservation days at right.

trousers until 1898. Even then it took force and persistence to do the job.

But the rest of the Apaches were quick to change once they could get cloth from the Spanish and Mexicans, either through trade or by forceful appropriation. Eventually Apache men began wearing a loosely fitting shirt of red, white, or gray cotton cloth, later of calico. The bottom of this long shirt fell well down over the tops of a pair of equally loose cotton drawers which came down to the knees.

There was another fashion shift in men's clothing in the 1870s. By that time some Apaches had added to their wardrobe such white men's garments as they had been able to lay their hands on. These included denim shirts, coats, vests, trousers, neckerchiefs, and even hats, particularly black derby hats, which were highly prized. But most Apaches still clung to their native high-topped buckskin moccasins.

Apache women's fashions also changed in the 1870s. They began to adopt the styles of the white women's dresses they saw on military posts, which many of them are still wearing today. A voluminous, ankle-length skirt made of ten to twenty yards of brightly colored cloth was topped by a high-necked, long-sleeved blouse made of equally brightly colored cloth. Basic to every costume, of course, were the inevitable high buckskin moccasins.

Soft deerskins were used as ponchos or blankets by both men and women in colder weather. Blankets were also obtained in raids or in trade from the Mexicans or from both the Navajo and Zuni Indians.

Both Apache men and women were fond of wearing ornaments —earrings, necklaces, bracelets, and pendants of shell, stone, and other materials. Turquoise was particularly prized, most of it being picked up from the ground around one of the hundreds of prehistoric Pueblo Indian ruins dotting the Apache landscape. Many of these were actually amulets or charms, worn primarily for their religious and protective value.

Apache
Social Life

APACHE social life revolved around the family, as it still does. The term family means a man and a woman and their children living in one house or wickiup. Two married couples rarely, if ever, lived in the same dwelling permanently.

Yet seldom do you see an Apache wickiup or house standing all by itself. In prereservation times such a sight would have been even rarer. The Apaches were, and still are, extremely gregarious. They needed close association with other families.

Apaches, in fact, seldom traveled anywhere alone. It was thought to be unsafe, not only because of enemies and dangerous wild animals but also because of the possibility of accidents and injury. Men generally hunted in pairs or in parties, while women out gathering wild plant foods always went in groups.

Although this picture has changed now, even as late as the 1930s there were grown men who had never spent a night alone. As one such man said, when he was caught out after dark and had to camp by himself, "It was a frightening experience. I hope I never have to go through it again." He went on to say that he had felt lonely and that the hooting of owls had kept him awake most of the night. Another man added, "It isn't right when people live all alone, not even a family."

Yet in spite of this feeling of gregariousness, an Apache camp was rarely a large one. The typical Apache camp cluster might be called an extended family, a family of relatives. This was generally made up of one elderly couple or a widow or widower, their unmarried sons and daughters, if any, their married daughters and their husbands and children, and occasionally a widowed relative or two or even a son-in-law's widowed parent.

The married sons normally didn't belong in the family group. Like many primitive and not so primitive people, most Apaches were matrilocal, which means that they followed the custom or belief that the husband should live with his wife's family group rather than with that of his own parents.

This doesn't mean that the Apache bride and groom moved in with the bride's family. In the first place, their wickiups just weren't that big. More importantly, however, an Apache husband could never look at or speak to his mother-in-law. The result was that the newlyweds built a new wickiup a short distance away from that of the bride's parents.

Matrilocal residence was not, however, always followed. A married son sometimes brought his wife and children to live with his parents rather than with his wife's family. Nor was it uncommon to find living in camp a son-in-law's widowed parent and even the widowed parent of a daughter-in-law. In spite of the usual tendency for a newly married husband to move next door to his wife's family, it was not uncommon for a son, particularly if he was an only son, to remain with his mother and sisters and bring his wife along with him.

In addition to being matrilocal, most Apaches were also matrilineal, tracing descent through the mother. Where we generally trace descent and relationship bilaterally, through the mother's and father's lines alike, many primitive peoples trace relationships on only one side of the family. While we make no distinction between an aunt or uncle or cousin on the mother's side of the family and an aunt or uncle or cousin on the father's side, that wasn't the way primitive people saw the family and its kinship relationships. An individual belonged either to his mother's family (matrilineal) or to his father's family (patrilineal), not to both.

This unilateral system of determining descent and relationship is one reason that you might have a hard time figuring out the typical Apache extended family. Containing as it does a large number of relatives which may, and often does, include three or four generations, tracking down who is related to whom can lead to some surprises.

The Chiricahua Apaches are an exception: they reckon descent bilaterally, treating maternal and paternal relatives more or less alike. However, since Chiricahua residence rules are matrilocal, maternal relatives naturally play a more important role in kinship behavior.

The number of separate dwellings or wickiups forming the extended family camp varied according to the number of married daughters of the original couple. Each daughter upon marriage occupied a separate dwelling with her husband. An adult unmarried son might have his own adjoining dwelling. Generally from three to seven or eight of these basic family households made up the average extended family camp, with a total population of from twelve to twenty individuals.

Many Apache camps were no larger than this. But generally, through close clan (a term to be explained later in this chapter) and other ties, several of these extended families built in the same locality, either in a good seed gathering and hunting area or around a farming site. This local group so formed was made up of from two to six or eight of these extended family camps. From thirty to a hundred people lived in the ten to thirty or more wickiups making up the local group.

Even when joined together in the local group village—if we can call such a loosely knit collection that—the extended family clusters still managed to retain their identities. The dwellings of each extended family were grouped together and set slightly apart from the others.

The extended family camp was the normal unit of everyday Apache life. Each household in the camp was a self-contained unit: its members lived in their own separate wickiup, cooked and ate at one fire, and made most of the implements and utensils that they used. But most other activities were shared by two or three households or by the entire extended family cluster.

The extended family bulked large in the daily life of the individ-

Coyote and his family, an example of a White Mountain Apache extended family about 1913.

WESTERN WAYS PHOTO BY E. EDGAR GUENTHER

ual Apache. It was the center for such day-to-day enterprises as hunting, seed gathering, and whatever farming they might do. Several Western Apache households would usually work a farm together and share in the harvest. Hunting and gathering parties were organized among extended family members, and the extended family moved as a whole during the summer and fall seasons when wild crops were collected. It is safe to say that Apaches spent most of their lives in the company of their relatives.

Yet there was also a great deal of intercourse between the several extended families making up the local group. Certain activities required cooperation of more people than there were in one extended family. Raiding parties, for example, were generally made up of people from the entire local group, as were large-scale hunts.

Most ceremonies also involved the local group and frequently even the band or several bands.

People of the same local group felt bound together by territorial association, blood, marriage, and close friendship. These ties separated them from the members of other local groups. Each local group was associated with a farming site or, if it did not farm, with some favorable valley or mountain location to which its members always returned. At this place there was longer continued residence than in any other area.

The still larger band was made up of a number of local groups. But the ties holding them together were more territorial than political. Each band had a name, generally a geographic name identifying it with its own fairly well defined territory within which the various local groups ranged in their yearly round of activities.

Since Apaches spent so much time with close kin, the manner in which they treated these relatives was important. This matter of kinship behavior is often difficult for most of us to understand as, beyond our immediate family, we meet and talk with outsiders rather than with relatives. Once a week, once a month, or perhaps only once a year do we get together with a number of other relatives. Yet the Apaches had almost daily contact not only with parents and brothers and sisters but also with grandparents, aunts and uncles, cousins of all degrees, and in-laws. Their behavior, rights, privileges, obligations, and choice of mates were all dictated by kinship.

In addition to membership in an extended family, every Western Apache and Navajo also belonged to another organization known as the clan. The other Apaches didn't have clans. The Navajos adopted the clan system from the Pueblo Indians, while the Western Apaches borrowed the idea either from the Pueblos or from the Navajos. This must have happened far back in the past, as most Western Apaches believe that they have always had clans.

Every Western Apache and Navajo boy and girl was born into one clan, that of his or her mother, and remained a member of that clan as long as he or she lived no matter where he or she went or whom he or she married. Every tribal member, male and female, belonged to one and only one clan. He or she didn't join a clan but was born into it. The Western Apaches, in fact, commonly classified by clan rather than by family. If asked what kind of a person another was, a Western Apache would answer by giving the name of the clan to which that individual belonged.

The clan was thus another unilateral kinship unit composed of people who considered themselves related through the maternal line and descendants of those ancestors who founded the clan's first farming site or settled at some specific geographic area. Each clan had a name which usually referred to this legendary place of origin. There were sixty-two Western Apache clans and some fifty to sixty Navajo clans, with such names as Bitter-Water, Grey-Earth-Place, Poles-Strung-Out, and Yucca-Blossom-Patch.

Certain Western Apache clans were thought of as related to each other and were grouped into one of three brotherhoods, each of which was thought to be descended from an archaic clan. Whether traceable or not, clan membership was considered blood relationship. Marriage was, therefore, prohibited between members of the same or closely related clans. Distantly related clan members were, however, permitted to marry.

The clan's main functions were to regulate marriage, extend kinship relations beyond the family, control farming or hunting sites, control rights to special ceremonies, and furnish the basis for war party organization. Clan members formed a tight-knit group within which there was a bond of obligation almost as close as that of the family. Clan members were expected to help each other whenever possible. Every member of an individual's clan or related clans was looked on as a relative, giving the individual more brothers and sisters and aunts and uncles not only in his or her own village but also in all other tribal villages, as clans were not limited territorially. This widely scattered membership helped tie the various extended families and local groups and bands closer together.

The strength of Apache society lay in the extended family. Directing this was a head man, a subchief. The prestige of the extended family depended primarily on the wealth and power of the subchief and secondarily on the strength of its clan ties.

The closest relatives an individual had were his blood brothers and sisters. The children of the mother's brother or the father's sister were grouped as cross-cousins, and the children of the mother's sister and father's brother as parallel cousins. The latter were called brothers and sisters and were treated in much the same manner as actual brothers and sisters.

Apache parents were proud and fond of their children. This was shown more in tolerance and interest than in lavish affection. Both male and female children were welcome. However, parents did not like a family of boys alone, as they felt the family line would die out. This is similar to our feeling about the family name dying out when only daughters are born.

Apache children were usually obedient and well behaved. Parents seldom if ever lost their tempers with children. Physical punishment was rare, children usually being handled by threats. There were few spoiled brats and no cry-babies, as crying children were ignored unless actually hurt. Children's later interests were tied more closely to the mother's side of the family due to matrilocal residence and, in the case of the Navajos and Western Apaches, to automatic membership in the mother's clan.

Apache society differed from ours in many ways. For example, it supplied no place for those who were unmarried. An adult male without a wife or an adult woman without a husband was to be pitied, even in some cases ridiculed. Failure to marry was very rare and considered abnormal and was almost an economic impossibility.

In prereservation times the average age at marriage was fifteen to eighteen for women, twenty to twenty-five for men. Young men could not get married quite as early because they first had to prove their ability to provide for a family by taking part in at least four raids. Marriage was as much or more an economic arrangement as it was a romantic affair.

Although marriage was usually arranged by the boy's parents, marriages which were the result of courtship were not uncommon. Unmarried girls were carefully guarded by relatives. Casual contact between the sexes was discouraged, and loose women were strongly disapproved of. But there were ways for young people attracted to each other to meet, particularly at ceremonial dances. Normally, a representative of the young man's family approached the woman's relatives. When an agreement had been reached, the

Baskets used in the wedding ceremony by the Navajo Indians. These baskets are now made for them by Ute and Southern Paiute Indians.

former presented the woman's family with a gift of from two to six horses, blankets, or guns in accordance with tribal etiquette. In return the bride's family reciprocated with gifts, though these were never as numerous.

Navajos held a wedding ceremony, called a basket ceremony, at the hogan of the bride's parents. The young couple ate cornmeal mush from a wedding basket of distinctive design, and the meal was followed by rituals and gift giving.

Other Apache couples began their married life without benefit of ceremony. As soon as a separate dwelling could be built next to that of the woman's parents, the couple moved in. For the first two or three months the bride did no cooking, bringing over food her mother had prepared.

The bridegroom had certain duties and obligations to his new relatives. He was expected to work for his parents-in-law, filling the economic gap created when their own sons married and moved away. He had to use special terms for different classes of relatives.

Some he could joke with; others he had to treat with respect.

But above all an Apache or Navajo man had to avoid his mother-in-law. The two could not look at each other, speak directly to each other, or be in the same room at the same time. The mother-in-law couldn't even see her daughter get married. If any of these events did happen, supernatural powers would, Navajos thought, cause blindness. This behavior pattern was supposed to show the deep respect the two had for each other.

To prevent a man and his mother-in-law from seeing each other, the two houses were usually built so that the entrances were not in sight of each other. When a woman knew her son-in-law was outside, she was careful to keep out of sight, and he did the same for her. A woman who accidentally met her son-in-law would throw her blanket over her head and turn away. The man would also face the other way and hurry off in the opposite direction. If a woman wanted to visit her daughter's house while her son-in-law was still there, she would send word so that the man might leave.

An Apache man also held his father-in-law in marked respect. Although they might occasionally speak to each other in a reserved manner, the father-in-law frequently told his daughter what he wanted, even when he knew her husband was within hearing. These behavior patterns, including similar avoidance or respect shown other of the wife's relatives, were extremely important in Apache society and were strictly observed in almost all cases.

Some Apache and Navajo men even had the problem of trying to avoid two mothers-in-law, but this didn't happen too often. The average man had all he could do to support one woman, and the practice of having more than one wife was largely confined to wealthy individuals, chiefs or subchiefs. Some Indians who wanted a second wife neatly sidestepped the difficulty of avoiding two mothers-in-law by marrying sisters.

Each of a husband's wives and her children occupied a separate wickiup. Generally the husband kept his personal belongings in the first wife's dwelling, and the first wife was the recognized leader of the camp, directing the work of the other women.

Most people have the mistaken idea that Indians lacked true affection. Most of the things we think show affection, as kissing, holding hands, and embracing in public, the Apaches considered either disgusting or improper. They simply showed their affection in ways other than public demonstrations.

Divorce was simple. Since the woman owned the house, all she had to do was stack her husband's personal belongings outside under a tree. When he returned and saw his saddle and other things outside, he knew what it meant and went home to his mother. If a man wanted to divorce his wife, he might tell her he was going hunting and just not return. Sometimes, to get rid of an unwelcome husband, a woman created an excuse by nagging him until he beat her, giving her good reason to leave him. Jealousy, incompatability, or failure of either to fulfill the duties of family life were the principal causes of divorce. Either could remarry immediately. A single young adult just didn't fit into the social and economic pattern of Apache society.

The husband of an unfaithful wife was expected to take some action. He might whip her, cut off the tip of her nose, or even kill her. A woman frequently sent an unfaithful husband away.

Wealth was gauged in terms of property—the horses and cattle secured in raids, the meat and hides and food supplies stored away. Being rich entailed a responsibility toward the poor: a rich person was supposed to be generous with his wealth.

To be brave meant not to be afraid of anything but at the same time to possess the judgment to look out for oneself in any situation. The person who blindly and fearlessly ran into trouble was a fool, rather than brave. The Apaches valued speed, endurance, and wiriness more highly than brute strength. To tell a deliberate lie was, to the Apaches, to commit a sin.

The Apache woman enjoyed a position in society far greater than might be supposed. She could and did own property and had a voice in family affairs. Even on local group councils she was frequently consulted. Family descent was traced through her line. She could and often did become a shaman or medicine woman. Victorio's sister, Lozen, was actually a warrior and greatly admired by her people.

There was no organized leadership for an entire band, let alone the whole tribe. The local group was the basic social, economic, and military body. This was the largest unit that had a definite leader.

A Chiricahua Apache woman with the end of her nose cut off as punishment for unfaithfulness.

The local group leader or chief had considerable power within his own group. He decided when it was time to return to the farming site and when it was time to plant and harvest. He organized food gathering trips and other economic enterprises. He determined when to send out raiding parties and when to put on one of the big ceremonials. However, a chief's authority was based mainly on influence, not absolute right. His position was that of an adviser, a councillor. He was obeyed only as long as his directions were effective.

A chief who had a reputation for success in hunting and raiding and for good leadership attracted families from other, less prosperous groups. This was particularly true for the Western Apaches where the local group chief was also the clan chief of his own clan. In this tribe chieftainship of all the large local groups was hereditary, remaining within the clan. It was limited, therefore, to maternal relatives of the preceding chief. Commonly a blood brother of the old chief, a son of the mother's sister, or a sister's son would inherit the office.

Among the Chiricahuas and other Apaches chieftainship of the local group was not necessarily hereditary. The leader was a man distinguished as an outstanding warrior and hunter. Although family origin did not always determine political rank, normally the leader came from the well born and wealthy. Yet his right to the position had to be backed up by achievement and effort. At the same time it was expected that a leader's son or a close relative would succeed as chief.

A chief's dwelling was generally larger than those of other people. His social position entitled him to respect from his people as well as from those outside the local group. Farm work and camp work on raiding and war parties were beneath his dignity. The chief who led a raiding party always received the largest share of booty. A warrior might receive three head of stolen stock, a sub-chief nine or ten, and the leader fifteen or twenty.

Whenever the several local groups in a band joined together for raiding or war, the most dominating leader of the local groups headed the combined band. This was particularly true for the Chiricahuas, where all local groups looked to Cochise as their leader.

A head chief remained in office as long as he was physically and mentally fit. When the time came, influential members of the local group chose the new chief. Often that was the occasion for a ceremony, including songs, ritual, feasting, and dancing. The new chief, if young, usually went through a period of training by an older man.

Under the head chief were a number of subchiefs, the heads of extended families, who were called rich men or strong men. Families varied in status and wealth, and only the most influential family heads attained the rank of subchief. This position was not hereditary or elective. Individuals gained the title through their own success in hunting and war, through wisdom in speech, through generosity, and through the strong backing of relatives. The authority of a subchief was restricted to his own local group and mainly within his own extended family. Subchiefs talked to the people, advising them how to live and take care of their families. They organized small hunting and gathering trips and sometimes led war parties. Most chiefs and subchiefs seldom let an opportunity pass to exhibit their oratorical ability.

Often the wives of chiefs and subchiefs were known as women chiefs or rich or strong women. They coordinated the activities of the women, organized food-gathering parties, and encouraged the women by setting good examples in storing food and making household utensils. The wives of headmen were almost as important and had almost as much authority as their husbands. Sometimes they spoke at war dances to encourage the men, and occasionally they spoke at chief's councils.

In most local groups one or two subchiefs were known as war leaders or war chiefs. They were men who were good fighters and had special war powers. They organized and directed the rituals and ceremonies connected with war parties. Thus, in any local group there were usually several different types of chiefs—head men or true chiefs, subchiefs, women chiefs and war chiefs.

Crime was not unknown in Apache society. Crimes included theft, destruction of property, injury to others, either accidental or intentional, trespass upon farming lands, incest, rape, murder, and witchcraft. Each of these was settled in its own way.

Theft was uncommon. It was said that only the poor stole, and the typical incident was a woman stealing corn from another woman's food cache or field. These were considered women's quarrels and left to them to settle, generally by the return of the stolen food. Occasionally a horse or cow was stolen. If the affair could not be settled, a subchief or other influential person was asked to arbitrate the dispute.

Damage to farm crops by stock breaking into fields was settled according to a recognized code. Upon payment of a blanket or buckskin or something of like value, the owner received the animal back. In rare cases an influential person was called in to settle the matter.

Accidental injuries caused by shooting or being kicked by another's horse could be atoned for by payment of a buckskin, blanket, or quiver. For accidentally caused deaths the payment was higher. Intentional injury, as in a fight, could also be settled by payment to avoid retaliation. The immediate relatives of those concerned would talk it over and agree on the compensation.

Murder was not uncommon in prereservation days. Most killings were the result of arguments during or following drinking parties. When an Apache fought, he usually fought to kill and frequently did. Murder could be settled by payment, thus avoiding a blood feud. Payments varied according to the social status of the victim, a wealthy or influential person requiring a higher compensation than a poor one. The maternal kinsmen of the murderer made the payment, piling up goods before the offended family until the amount was sufficient. The family sometimes burned the payment on the spot or sometimes took it home for use. In rare instances when a murder was so brutal and inexcusable that even the killer's relatives couldn't condone it, they gave him to the victim's family to kill on sight. This avoided revenge being taken on the other relatives. Yet even then payment still had to be made to the murdered man's family. In some cases when compensation failed the two families began a blood feud which might last for years, with first a killing on one side and then one on the other.

Young unmarried Apache women were brought up under a strict code. Unwelcome male attentions, even as slight as laying a hand on a woman's shoulder or foot, were offenses which could lead to trouble. If the woman complained to her parents or close relatives, they could demand payment or destroy property of the offender, slashing a buckskin to pieces or killing a horse. The culprit, knowing himself to be in the wrong, had to submit to this. Such incidents through varying degrees of intimacy to rape could be atoned for by payment. If the victim of a rape became pregnant, her parents usually insisted on the guilty man marrying her.

This custom of compensation for injuries was so well established that it was occasionally taken advantage of. A young divorced woman would lead a man into committing familiarities. She then would complain to her family about his unwarranted advances. The woman's relatives, as dishonest as she, would kill the man's horse and take the meat for their own use. The dupe submitted meekly rather than have other people find out how he had been taken in. This practice tended to make many a young man think twice before he made an advance.

Two major crimes, witchcraft and incest, were closely linked in Apache culture. Witches were thought to practice incest and therefore persons caught in incest were considered witches. Witchcraft was believed to cause illness and even death. Witches were feared and shunned. These two offenses were almost the only cases tried by a chief, and the usual punishment was banishment or death.

The basis for the Apache code of law was expressed in Apache terms as "getting even." Thus, you got even for an injury or murder by being paid or by killing a member of the offender's family.

11

Rituals, Medicine Men, and Ceremonies

APACHES were and still are deeply religious. The term religion, however, doesn't mean quite the same thing to Apaches as it does to us.

Among Apaches, as among other southwestern Indian tribes, there was no line separating religion from economic and social life. Practically everything in Apache life—planting, harvesting, fighting, hunting, building a house, making a bow or a basket, birth, death, sickness, accidents, even the weather—had its ritual or magical aspect. An Apache literally ate and slept and worked and played with religion every hour of the day and every day of the year.

Nor did Apache religion mean a church building, with a congregation, ministers, hymnbooks, and all the other features of one of our well-organized churches today. They did have prayers, chants, fasting, offerings, and the like. But they also had other religious items and activities which most of us might consider odd or unusual—mythological beings, spirits, ghosts, masked dancers, magic and magical formulas, fortune-telling, ceremonial smoking, color symbolism, sacred numbers, charms, purification rites, sweat baths, curing ceremonies, fear of the dead, medicine men, witches, to name only a few.

Apaches and Navajos shared similar mythologies of their origin, their heroes, and their gods and goddesses. Western Apache myths mentioned a legendary place far to the north where they lived long ago with the Navajo, Hopi, and Zuni Indians. Navajos, Western Apaches, and some other Apaches believed that they originally emerged from an underworld, an idea probably borrowed from the Pueblo Indians.

Apache mythology credited Yusn, the Giver of Life, as the source of all power and the creator of the universe. One of the most important Apache heroes was the goddess, White Painted Woman. From the union of White Painted Woman and the Sun came the twin heroes, Slayer of Monsters (also called Killer of Enemies) and Child of Water. There were also two varieties of water beings. One kind, the Controller of Water, was good, bringing rain; the other, the Water Monster, who sometimes appeared as a huge serpent, was bad, causing drownings.

An important series of Apache myths told about the Mountain People, supernatural beings believed to inhabit caves and mountain tops. In ancient times these Mountain People lived on the earth as people. Because of sickness and death, they finally left to search for a place of eternal life. These Mountain Spirits, called Gan, were thought to have power over human beings, either to help them or to harm them, according to how one approached the Mountain Spirits. The Apaches, therefore, held the Gan in both fear and reverence. Masked and costumed Apache dancers impersonate or represent the Gan during certain ceremonies. (These are the dancers often erroneously called Devil or Crown Dancers.)

The Navajos also had their gods and goddesses, the Holy People, powerful and mysterious beings. Changing Woman, the favored figure among the Holy People, was the counterpart of the Apache White Painted Woman. Changing Woman and her husband, the Sun, were the parents of the hero twins, Slayer of Monsters and Child of the Water. The adventures of these twin war gods served as models of conduct for aspiring young Navajo warriors. Other Navajo deities included the Yeis, male and female spirits representing the forces of nature—clouds, rain, wind, thunder, lightning.

Another series of Apache and Navajo tales dealt with Coyote, a buffoon and trickster, who was considered responsible for most of

Western Apache masked Gan dancers performing during the coming out ceremony for girls.

humanity's troubles including lying, gluttony, theft, adultery, and death. Mescaleros, however, said he stole fire from the flies and gave it to humans. Such stories were often told the young people to teach moral lessons.

One of the most important individuals in Apache and Navajo society was the medicine man or shaman. These were people who had received power from a supernatural source, giving them capabilities above and beyond their own resources. We call it supernatural power because we distinguish between natural and supernatural forces. But Apaches don't make this distinction. To them powers, gods and goddesses, ghosts, and the like are just as real as the sun or wind or rain. The source of this inexhaustible power lay in certain birds, snakes, and other animals and forces of nature.

An Apache could obtain power in several different ways, either through a dream or some unusual or unexpected event or by buying it from a shaman. Theoretically every Apache could get power. But the majority didn't because learning the appropriate chants and prayers and rituals from a particular power involved years of hard work and money. One noted Navajo medicine man studied for twenty-six years before he held his first nine-day ceremony. Furthermore, possession of power not only brought on responsibilities, but also frequently incited fear and jealousy in other people.

Shamans used power primarily to diagnose and cure illness. Other individuals who had power, generally through purchase, used it for more personal needs such as finding lost objects, insuring success in everything from hunting and war to love and gambling, controlling the weather, and predicting future events.

Most shamans were older men. There were, however, a number of women shamans, and some of them were as powerful as men shamans. Yet women were mainly concerned with minor ceremonials or parts of major ones.

Apache and Navajo shamans were usually excellent showmen and sleight-of-hand experts. To show the power of his supernatural helper, a Mescalero Apache shaman made feathers disappear. Navajo medicine men impressed their audiences by swallowing arrows, performing juggling tricks, and making feathers dance in a basket. Every shaman had his medicine bag of sacred paraphernalia, which might include cattail pollen, paints, herbs, eagle feathers, quartz crystals, red ocher, and tobacco. Some Apache medicine men wore a cap of buckskin decorated with eagle or raven feathers and turquoise.

While most shamans would tackle any kind of problem, their main task was to diagnose and cure illness. To a Navajo or Apache sickness, like death, was not a natural event. With few exceptions all ailments, both physical and mental, were due to one of three things: the evil power of a witch or sorcerer, contact with a ghost, or the deliberate or accidental violation of one or more taboos, such as stepping on the trail left in the dust by a snake or using wood from a tree struck by lightning to make a fire or drinking water from a creek in which a bear had been swimming. Taboos of this kind ran far up in the hundreds.

Ceremonial buckskin.

Once the exact cause of the ailment was determined through divination, then the medicine man knew which of the numerous ceremonies to use to effect a cure. Navajos had forty or fifty of these curing ceremonies, popularly called chants or ways, each from one to nine days in length. The Shooting Chant counteracted the magic of lightning and thunder and arrows, while the Bead Chant cured skin diseases. Each ceremony was an elaborate affair involving songs, prayers, sacred pollen, prayer sticks, rattles, offerings, dances, herbs and medicines, emetics, sweat baths, and sand paintings.

One of the most colorful features of Navajo curing ceremonies was the sand paintings or dry paintings. There were more than 500 of these symbolic representations of Navajo mythology, each linked to a particular chant. Made of ground minerals, sandstone, charcoal, and pollen, they ranged from one to twenty feet in diameter, with the larger ones taking the medicine man and a dozen assistants nearly all day to complete. Like the songs, prayers, and other rituals, the pattern of each sand painting was carried in the

Navajo sand painting made on the floor of a hogan for the sick man lying to the left.

mind of the medicine man and was handed down from one medicine man to another. The sand painting was made and destroyed between sunrise and sunset of the same day, its ceremonial burial ridding the patient of the sickness, which was absorbed by the sand.

Other Apache curing ceremonies were not as elaborate as Navajo chants. But most of them followed the same general pattern and included songs, prayers, ceremonial smoking, sacred pollen, masked dancers, and sand paintings. The latter, however, were made only by the Jicarilla and Western Apaches and were neither as complicated nor as numerous as those of the Navajo.

Most Navajo and other Apache medicine men performed rituals and ceremonies in accordance with a definite directional order. With few exceptions they began a ritual act at the east, and proceeded clockwise to the south and then the west, ending up at the north. An Apache shaman, for example, would smoke a ceremonial cigarette and puff smoke out to the four directions, beginning with the east and going clockwise to end at the north. The use of color in a curing or other ceremony also followed a regular symbolic directional pattern. For most Apaches this was black for the east, blue for the south, yellow for the west, and white for the north. Navajo medicine men, however, used black for the north, white for the east, blue for the south, and yellow for the west. To Navajos, black was the color of evil, of disease and trouble, while white was the source of good. Navajos associated their color directions with sacred jewels—white crystal with the east, blue turquoise with the south, yellow abalone shell with the west, and black coal with the north.

The Navajos even applied sex distinctions to color and directions as well as to wind and rain and to almost anything which had an opposite. To them the black north was male, the blue south female; cold winds were male, warm winds female; lightning and thunder and heavy storms were male, soft rains female. Chiricahua Apaches also had sex distinctions for rain, calling a heavy, pouring rain male and a light shower female. Masks representing a Navajo god were round, those of a goddess square.

Apaches and Navajos also believed there was magic in numbers. Four was the sacred or lucky number for both Navajos and Apaches and for practically all other southwestern Indians. Nearly everything in their ceremonies—prayers, songs, dances, smoking, ritual acts—went in sets of four. Many of the ceremonies themselves were four-day or four-night ones.

At the conclusion of an Apache curing ceremony, the shaman almost invariably imposed a food or behavior taboo upon the patient. Frequently he gave the patient a curative or protective amulet to wear. A lightning or snake shaman might give the patient a painted buckskin to ward off further evil.

Most Navajo and Apache curing ceremonies were expensive affairs, particularly if they were lengthy ones. The chief medicine man and his assistants had to be paid and generally well paid. Today a Navajo medicine man may receive up to 500 dollars or more or the equivalent in goods. In addition, all the Indians attending the ceremonial had to be fed. For a nine-day chant, this item alone could run high.

Outstanding shamans commanded respect similar to that given to chiefs. Because of their control over social, economic, and religious events, they often had an even stronger influence than chiefs. People listened to what they had to say on almost any subject. Jicarilla Apaches thought that mountains and rivers, even the sun and moon, were brought into existence by their medicine men. Families frequently moved from one group to another just to be near a good medicine man who could be depended upon in times of evil or illness.

In prereservation days most Apaches were fond of games and gambling. Most of their games of chance and skill involved some ceremonialism. Their chief games were a hidden ball game, a three-stick dice game, and a hoop and pole game. The hoop and pole game was for men only; women weren't allowed to go anywhere near the hoop and pole field. Even the dogs were kept away from the area when the men were playing.

Not all Navajo and Apache ceremonies were curing ceremonies. The Western Apaches, Navajos, and Jicarillas had many minor ceremonies for the planting, growing, and harvesting of crops. To bring rain for their planted fields, Western Apaches held a lightning ceremony in early summer, in which two boys and two girls or four boys and four girls danced at night with hoops or crossed poles. Often there was a ceremony upon the completion of a new wickiup.

Navajos also had a few special ceremonies for rain making,

Western Apache girl's coming-out ceremony, with the girl lying on a pile of skins and blankets in back of baskets of food and other things to be given away.

hunting, war, trading, gambling, and salt gathering. One of the most frequently performed Navajo chants was the Blessing Way Chant, given to keep people well, to insure their continued health, wealth, and good fortune, and to keep the family in tune with the Holy People. The Blessing Way Chant was given for girls when they came of age, for pregnant women, for marriage ceremonies, for men going off to war or returning, for a family after a death had occurred, or whenever the need was felt for good luck. You might call the Blessing Way Chant a precautionary or protective measure, not an actual cure for anything.

In addition, most Navajo curing ceremonies included secondary ceremonies. During the last two nights of the nine-day Night Way Chant masked representatives of the Yeis put on initiation rites for boys and girls between the ages of seven and thirteen. The so-called Squaw Dance, primarily a coming-out party for eligible young women, took place on the last night of the three-day Enemy Way Chant. One of the most spectacular Navajo ceremonies, an

Western Apache girls standing under the ceremonial tipi during their coming-out ceremony.

WESTERN WAYS PHOTO BY CHARLES W. HERBERT

elaborate purification ritual called the Fire Dance, furnished a dramatic climax for the nine-day Mountain Top Way. Practically all large Apache ceremonies, and sometimes marriages, were accompanied by all-night social dances at which the people of several local groups got together for feasting and dancing.

By far the most important and elaborate Apache ceremony was the puberty ritual for girls. This highly dramatic four-day ceremony marked the high point in the life of an Apache girl. In addition to its ritual significance, it was also an important social event, a time for dancing, singing, feasting, and gossiping. White Painted Woman was said to have established the puberty rite long, long ago. The girl going through the ceremony was even identified with White Painted Woman and called by that name during the four days and nights of the ritual and for the following four days.

These rituals were expensive affairs, as the young girl's family had to hire a shaman to conduct the ceremony, pay the masked dancers and others assisting, furnish vast quantities of food for the numerous friends and visitors who never passed up an opportunity to attend such a party and its related social events, and sometimes even furnish eagle feathers, baskets, skins, and other ritual objects for the medicine man. Since all this expense taxed the resources of any one family, two to four families with daughters about the same age would often put on the ceremony together so they could split the cost between them. This was the case in two such ceremonies the writer witnessed.

This was and still is one of the most colorful of all Apache ceremonials. The girls were dressed in new ceremonial buckskin clothing stained yellow, the color of sacred pollen, and decorated with symbols of the sun, moon, and stars. The ceremony included the construction of a ceremonial tipi (but not built in all Apache groups); a molding ritual in which each girl was massaged by a woman attendant to make her straight and supple and to insure her a good disposition; the sprinkling of sacred pollen; food taboos and certain behavior taboos, such as the use of a cane drinking tube to avoid touching water with the lips (or the girl would develop unsightly facial hair) and the use of a scratching stick instead of the fingernails (or the girl would have ugly facial sores and scars);

the throwing of a blanket, the traditional symbol of wealth, by the girl in each of the four directions, beginning with the east; ceremonial smoking; and lengthy chants sung by the shaman.

Perhaps the most colorful event was the nightly performance of the masked dancers, impersonators of the Gans, the Mountain Spirits. Numbering anywhere from four to sixteen, plus a clown or two for comic relief, these dancers wore yellow buckskin kilts, with the rest of their exposed bodies entirely covered with painted designs in black, white, and yellow. Their most imposing features were their awesome masks and high arching headdresses. Their dances blessed the gathering and drove away any evil which might upset the proceedings.

The ceremony ended on the fourth morning with a tipi ceremony, ceremonial foot race, the throwing of gifts to the spectators, and the ceremonial dismantling of the tipi.

The successful completion of the ceremony supposedly brought health and wealth and long life to the girl. All those attending the ceremony shared in the girl's blessing and good fortune. During this time and for a period of four days after the ceremony, the girl was believed to possess special curative powers. Before the ceremony she was still a girl. When it was over, she was a woman ready for marriage, ready to take her place in Apache society.

12

Witches
and
Ghosts

APACHES and Navajos were fervent believers in witches and ghosts and were equally fervent in their fear of both, as were most other southwestern Indians. Ghosts, of course, were the souls of the dead. As soon as an individual died, his soul left his body and became a ghost. Although ghosts were normally invisible and had supernatural powers, they still had the same emotions as the living. While an occasional ghost might be good, most ghosts were bad. Instead of heading directly for the spirit world, where they belonged, ghosts often hung around for some time spying on their former relatives and friends.

Some Navajo ghosts were great practical jokers. They loved to frighten people and to play pranks on them. Nothing seemed to make them happier than to chase people or throw dirt and rocks at them. Apache ghosts often did the same things.

If that were all that Navajo and Apache ghosts did, they wouldn't be too bad; but most ghosts didn't stop there. If ghosts weren't treated properly, they could get mad at the living and, through their supernatural power, cause misfortune, sickness, and even death. That's why Navajos and Apaches didn't like ghosts hanging around any longer than necessary.

Navajo and Apache fear of the dead and everything connected with them rested upon their fear of ghosts. Navajos believed that ghosts were the witches of the dead, evil beings who could return at any time from the spirit world to plague the living. No matter how kind and friendly dead persons may have been when they were alive, once they became ghosts—chindi, as the Navajos called them—they were potentially dangerous to the health, welfare, and even the lives of those who came in contact with them.

Navajos, therefore, never wasted any time in disposing of the dead. In former days Navajo slaves were given the unpleasant job of getting rid of the corpses, as Navajos didn't like to look at or handle the dead. In recent years if the relatives couldn't get white friends or neighbors to undertake the task, they selected four official mourners from the clan of the deceased to take charge of the funeral. After preparing the body, the burial attendants knocked a hole in the north wall of the hogan, the direction of evil and the afterworld, and carried the body out through it. Once outside they lost no time getting to the hole in the ground or the niche in the rocks where they could leave the body with its valuable possessions, which would insure the deceased an entrance into the afterworld.

Navajos also took elaborate precautions to make sure the deceased's ghost didn't come back to harm them. They tried to outwit the ghost by carefully brushing out their tracks to and from the grave and even returned by a different route. They could not look backward toward the grave, nor could they talk on the return trip. Then they either burned or tore down the hogan and never went near that spot again, ever hopeful that they had fooled the ghost.

Like the Navajos, Apaches didn't lose any time in disposing of the dead, burying them the same day they died whenever possible. They reduced to a minimum the time during which the living and the dead were in contact because they believed the dreaded ghost sickness could be caught from the dead, from the sight of the corpse, or from the possessions of the deceased. Burial was as far away as possible, either in the ground, with the deceased laid out full length, or in a crevice in the rock. Some personal belongings were buried with the dead, and a person's favorite horse was usually killed at his grave. The rest of his possessions, along with his wick-iup, were burned or destroyed, while the family immediately moved to a new site. This move might not be very far, only from one side of a field to the other. But this was thought to be enough to fool the ghost. To further fool the ghost, Apache relatives often changed their appearance by cutting their hair.

We visit cemeteries to put flowers on graves of relatives or close friends, but the Apaches never went near a grave. In fact, anyone hanging around a grave was suspected of being a witch. Even to think of the dead or to speak their names might bring their ghosts back, which would lead to the fatal ghost or darkness sickness. Both Navajos and Apaches had a period for mourning and fasting and purification rites.

To mention the name of the dead was taboo to both Navajos and Apaches. Because of contact with Anglos Apaches are today less hesitant about speaking the name of the dead, although they still dislike doing so. Yet, to show great respect for the dead, Apaches sometimes after fifteen years or more had passed named a child for some deceased member of his or her clan.

Apaches and Navajos had to be extremely careful what they said or did or the ghost would come back to take out its spite on its former relatives and friends. If a corpse hadn't been buried prop-erly or if some of his possessions hadn't been burned or buried with him or if his grave had been disturbed, the ghost would return to the grave or to his former hogan to avenge the neglect or offense.

Navajos also believed that bad dreams, dreams about a ghost and the like, were sent by ghosts who were trying to entice their relatives into ghostland. If these dreams recurred, the Navajos tore down their hogan and, to frustrate the ghosts, built a new hogan some distance away.

Navajo and Apache ghosts were usually out only at night. That's why Navajos don't like to go out alone at night. Unlike most ghosts these night ghosts sometimes showed up in human form. If a Chiricahua Apache saw such a ghost, he knew that he would die within a year. To Navajos, seeing a ghost or having one throw dirt or rocks at them were omens of coming disaster, the death of the individual who saw the ghost or the death of one of his rela-

Navajo Indian drawing a corn symbol on a sandstone rock already covered with prehistoric Indian petroglyphs.

TAD NICHOLS

tives. Only the proper ceremonial treatment could ward off death.

Whistling at night was always evidence that a ghost was not far away. Navajos never whistled after dark, as this would bring the evil spirits and some accident or bad luck would follow. If an Apache heard a whistle at night, he tossed some ashes in the direction of the sound to frighten the ghost away. Often a footprint in the ground was the only sign that a ghost had been around an Apache wickiup. Tracks like these usually led directly to graves.

Apache and Navajo ghosts could also appear in the form of owls. Apaches thought owls were the ghosts of individuals who had been bad during life and continued to be bad after death. Mescaleros believed that the owl represented the spirit or ghost of a dead witch. Navajos never killed owls, as anyone who did would become blind. Both Apaches and Navajos interpreted the hooting of an owl as a forewarning of imminent trouble, of possible sickness or death. If an owl hooted above a Navajo hogan the famliy living there would soon learn of the illness or death of a relative. If a Chiricahua heard an owl, he knew that a ghost was not far away. To Chiricahuas owls were dangerous. They were afraid to say anything about owls, or tell stories about them, or to throw anything at them. When an owl flew past a Chiricahua, it was a sign that someone was going to die. To keep their children quiet and out of mischief, Chiricahua mothers would tell them that the wicked owl would catch them if they were bad.

Witches, however, were different. To Navajos and Apaches, as well as to most other southwestern Indians, witches were persons who possessed special power to do evil. Unlike ghosts, witches were real people, looking just as pleasant and kindly as one's next-door neighbor. Yet, through their alliance with malignant spirits of the supernatural world, witches could do things no ordinary mortal could.

Witchcraft wasn't quite the same thing as magic. Usually witchcraft didn't require any magical aids; a witch could deal out sickness and death just by wishing. Sometimes witches used magic spells, charms, and medicine to bring misfortune to others. Some Apache Indians called these professionals who used black magic sorcerers, not witches. But whatever they called them, most Indians recognized that both witches and sorcerers were evil and didn't want to have anything to do with them.

Witches and sorcerers learned their art from already established practitioners. Since witches were naturally reluctant to pass on their secrets to anyone who wasn't a close maternal kinsman, certain clans or related clans became topheavy with sorcerers. Nor did witchcraft come cheaply. Students had to pay heavily to learn the techniques of doing in their fellow tribesmen.

Among southwestern Indians both men and women could be witches, although in some tribes, such as the Navajo and Apache, most witches were men. A survey made in the 1940s revealed that out of a total of 222 Navajos accused of witchcraft, only 38 were women.

Both Navajos and Apaches took their witchcraft and black magic seriously. Mescalero, Chiricahua, and Western Apaches thought that nearly all of life's ills and accidents were the work of witches or evil sorcerers.

Like ghosts, Navajo and Apache witches were active primarily at night. Navajos and Apaches were even more afraid of witches than they were of ghosts, perhaps because witches could cause a great deal more misfortune and sickness than ghosts could. Navajo witches, so Navajos believed, all belonged to a witch's society. The initiation fee was the killing of a close relative, preferably a brother or a sister. At their secret meetings, held in caves or abandoned hogans and presided over by a chief witch, they danced and chanted, made plans for action against future victims, feasted on the corpses of victims killed by fellow witches to acquire some of the supernatural power possessed by ghosts, and initiated new members. When roving around at night on business, witches disguised themselves as werewolves, dressing in the skins of wolves, coyotes, foxes, bears, or owls. They could travel, either on the ground or through the air, with supernatural speed. Sometimes they left tracks like those of their animal disguises, but considerably larger.

Although a Navajo witch could injure or kill by evil thoughts alone, he could also kill by uttering spells over an image of the intended victim or something closely associated with him, such as hair or nail clippings or a fragment of clothing, which the witch hid in a grave. Or the witch might magically shoot into the victim something connected with corpses, like bits of bone or some ashes from a hogan in which someone had died. But a Navajo witch's most powerful weapon was corpse poison, a concoction made from dried and ground up human flesh, preferably that of children. The witch might give this poison powder to the potential victim in his food or cigarettes or drop it into his hogan through the smokehole or blow it in his face, usually at a night ceremony.

Navajo witches not only injured or killed people to satisfy their envy or need for vengeance, but they also carried out their witchcraft and black magic against animals, crops, and personal property. Today even an auto might be bewitched. Nor was this all that Navajo witches did. One witch went into partnership with a medicine man, the witch making a person ill and the medicine man curing him; the two of them would then split the fee. Witches often made their living by robbing graves of the turquoise and silver jewelry and other valuable offerings left with the dead.

This might sound as if Navajo witches could get away with almost anything, even with murder. Navajos might fear witches, but they did not meekly stand by and let witches do what they wanted. Certain plants and animals were believed to give protection against witches. One of the best of these was gall medicine, made from the gall (the fluid secreted by the liver) of bears, eagles, mountain lions, or skunks. Careful Navajos never went out without taking their gall medicine along. If witchcraft hadn't gained too strong a hold on its victim, curing was possible through certain antiwitchcraft ceremonials. The Evil Way Chant, for example, was useful against both ghost troubles and witchcraft.

But perhaps the best protection against witchcraft was to find out which witch had been doing the dirty work. A suspected Navajo witch was given a chance to confess. If he wouldn't, he might be tied down and not allowed to eat or drink until he did confess. This caused the witchcraft to backfire, the victim getting well while the witch himself got sick and died. If a witch didn't confess, he was often killed, and sometimes he was killed even if he did confess, following the principle, one would assume, that a dead witch was a good witch.

Since witches and sorcerers worked only at night, Navajos never ground corn or swept the hogan floor at night, so as to avoid all suspicion of being a witch or dealing in black magic. In fact, anyone who acted mean or threatening in a Navajo community was likely to be considered a witch.

Apache Indians thought the same way. If an Apache made a threat against another and it came true, he might be suspected of being a witch. Any Chiricahua caught hanging around a grave was suspected of being a witch. Any Chiricahua or Mescalero who did something peculiar might fall under suspicion of witchcraft. People who stole or did mean things were also thought to be witches.

Apache witches and sorcerers operated much like their Navajo counterparts. Some used poison powder to kill their victims, putting it in their food or throwing it through the door of the wickiup. Others used spell sorcery, either by just thinking evil thoughts about the victim or by casting spells, which might be repeated four times. To make the spell even more effective, the sorcerer would circle the victim's wickiup four times or place a piece of wood at each of the cardinal points around the dwelling. Spells could also be cast against crops, livestock, or other belongings of the intended victim.

To combat sorcery sickness, a medicine man performed one of several curing ceremonies, such as the bear or snake or lightning ceremonials. If he was successful, the sorcerer himself would die within a short time, and his victim would begin to recover.

Some Apache witches were said to practice shooting sorcery, shooting arrowlike missiles into the bodies of their victims. They could shoot these unerringly so far and so fast that they became invisible in the air and were scarcely felt by the victim. Their favorite arrows were strands of human hair, charcoal, bits of wood, pebbles, and pieces of human bone. Some Mescalero witches preferred live arrows—lizards, beetles, crickets, spiders, and stinging insects.

To cure such sorcery victims some Apache shamans specialized in blowing away the disease in the four directions. But most Chiricahua and Mescalero medicine men used the standard witchcraft treatment: they extracted by sleight-of-hand the witchcraft substance—a pebble, fragment of bone, or insect—from the patient's body by massaging or by applying suction with the mouth or a hollow cane tube. The medicine man then spat the object into the fire, where it exploded with a loud pop, a sure sign that the witchcraft missile had been destroyed.

Fighting witchcraft was, however, a dangerous business for all concerned. If the opposing witch was more powerful than the medicine man, the medicine man himself might die. Like the Navajos, most Apaches carried some sort of protection against sorcery —turquoise beads, cattail pollen, eagle feathers, and the like. An accused witch or sorcerer, on the other hand, stood alone. Since sorcery, unlike murder or theft, was a public crime, a witch's relatives couldn't help him.

One other form of magic was sometimes closely linked with witchcraft. This was love magic, which might be considered either good magic or bad magic, depending on whether the object of the magical wooing was single or not. Some Western Apaches even called those who practiced love magic love witches.

When Chiricahua, Mescalero, and Jicarilla Apaches wanted to cast a love spell on someone, they turned to specialists who knew love magic. These love magicians supposedly got their power from butterflies, hummingbirds, caterpillars, and deer. To most Mescaleros and Jicarillas, however, love magic lay on the borderline between good magic and witchcraft, as its aim was to influence another individual, generally against that individual's will, rather than to cure or help. Yet these same Apaches didn't want to speak too harshly against love magic, as many of them either had made use of love magic or intended to at some future time.

Navajos also believed love magic to be closely associated with witchcraft. In fact, they even called it Frenzy Witchcraft. Their magic love potion consisted of datura and poison ivy and three or four other plants. These plants had to be gathered in a certain manner, with special songs and prayers for each. Either the plant pollen or the powdered leaves and roots could be used, working through food or in cigarettes or simply by contact. Through the right prayers, it was said that Frenzy Witchcraft could be made to work over a distance of several hundred miles. According to most Navajos, Frenzy Witchcraft was strong medicine, often making women go crazy and tear their clothes off. One could, so it was said, even kill with Frenzy Witchcraft. It may originally have been used as a magical technique for obtaining foreign women. If a Navajo didn't want to use Frenzy Witchcraft as love magic, he could always use it to bring him success in gambling, in trading, or in hunting.

13

Raiding
and
Warfare

T O the Apache, raiding and warfare were as different as night
and day. In native terminology, raiding literally meant "to
hunt out enemy property," while warfare meant "to take
death from an enemy." Thus raiding had as its primary objective the stealing of enemy goods, preferably livestock. Any fighting that took place was purely accidental. With warfare, on the
other hand, fighting to avenge the death of a relative who had lost
his life in battle was the chief objective. Yet even war parties
brought back what plunder they could lay their hands on, often
including captives.

Raiding rivaled hunting in its economic importance to the local
group. To many Apaches it was either raid or starve. When food
supplies ran low, out they would go on a raiding party. Though
many chiefs and warriors achieved glory and a high status through
participation in successful raids, these attainments were only inci-
dental to the securing of booty.

Most raiding parties were small, formed from as few as five or
six men up to as many as ten or fifteen, all generally from a single
local group. There was little ceremony connected with raiding,
although it was usually desirable to include in the party an indi-

vidual who had war power. Raiders took very little with them, living off the land on the way to their target and off their plunder on the way back. Since the success of a raid depended upon not being spotted and not having to fight, they were careful to keep under cover both going and coming. When they were close to their selected target, they followed a number of taboos, including the use of a special warpath language. The raid itself usually took place in the early morning hours, with the Apaches striking swiftly and silently and leaving just as swiftly. Speed was a necessity on the journey home. Returning raiders sometimes went without sleep for as many as four or five days.

After a successful Navajo attack, the leader drew four symbolic lines in the sand with a flint arrowhead. These lines were charged with magical power to prevent the enemy from overtaking the party.

Raids were used as training for boys, who were trained for raiding and warfare just as thoroughly as today's athlete trains for a football game or a track meet. After a strenuous round of activities designed to harden and toughen a youngster, he was allowed to go on a raid. But for his first four raids he was merely an observer performing camp chores—building fires, gathering wood and water, cooking, taking care of the horses. He also had to follow a number of food and behavior taboos, such as carrying a special stick with which to scratch himself if he itched and a cane drinking tube, as water was not supposed to touch his lips. After his fourth raid the boy was considered a warrior and could take part in raids and war parties.

The Apaches did not organize raids to add more land to Apacheria or to drive away or kill off all Mexicans and others living in and around their territory. Quite the opposite was true. They did not destroy whole villages and people because they looked on these as valuable economic reservoirs which would through the years furnish substantial amounts of food and livestock for raiding Apaches. You might say that they believed that Mexicans existed solely to provide them with the things they needed. All outsiders, including the White Eyes, were enemies and could be preyed upon without scruple.

Nor did most Apaches, with the possible exception of some of

Western Apache war charm necklace.

ARIZONA STATE MUSEUM

the Plains Apaches, think that vainglorious exhibitions of courage were necessary. They took the realistic view that the most successful raider was the one who gained the greatest pile of loot with the least damage to himself. Admiration and praise went to the man who brought home the plunder, not to the dead hero who was not smart enough to get away.

War parties were formed primarily on the basis of clan relationship. It was the responsibility not only of a warrior's immediate relatives, but also of his clan brothers, to avenge his death. Such a war party might be composed of 100 or more men under the direction of a single leader.

Unlike raids, warfare was always accompanied by a great deal of ceremony. The Apaches were never more religious than when preparing for war; that was one time when they needed all the gods on their side. There was a war dance before leaving, to enlist the aid of the supernatural spirits, and a victory dance upon return. One or more medicine men who had war power usually went along with a war party. Each warrior carried a small buckskin bag of sacred meal for morning and evening sacrifice. Many carried protective amulets such as quartz crystals, pieces of petrified wood, sandstone concretions, or galena. Some wore buckskin shirts with painted designs believed to protect the wearer. Others wore protective buckskin war caps ornamented with eagle feathers. Most also carried more practical items such as buckskin awl cases with sinew and rawhide to repair wornout moccasins and tweezers to pluck out stray beard hairs. One or two would have a fire drill kit in their quiver cases.

As late as the 1850s and 1860s most of the Apaches were armed only with bows and arrows, spears, clubs, and knives. Though they had long known about guns and had picked up many through trade or by more direct action, these often became useless because of breakage or lack of ammunition. Having neither the means nor the knowledge to repair them, the Apaches put the broken parts to use as spears or knives. Not until the 1870s, when they were placed on reservations and many of them became scouts, did they procure plenty of guns and ammunition.

Apache success in war was due to their knowledge of the country and their ability to take care of themselves under any circum-

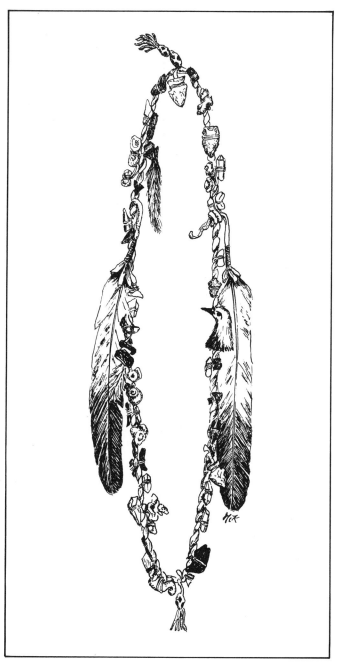

White Mountain war necklace worn over right shoulder and under left arm as a charm to ward off enemy blows, and for good luck at home. Decorated with quartz crystals, chalcedony, obsidian, projectile points, red beans, feathers, and a yellow bird's head.

stance. They could hide behind a rock, a bush, or even a clump of bear grass. They traveled light, living off the country as they moved. They found food and water in the desert and mountains where the average white person would starve to death or die of thirst. If they couldn't find food, they went without, often for days at a time. And they traveled fast. It was nothing to cover forty or fifty miles a day on foot, even more on horseback.

Battle-hardened American troops, bloodied in the Civil War and no strangers to hardship, found themselves handicapped rather than helped by their superior arms and equipment. The Apaches demonstrated that a brave but ill-armed foe could wreak havoc in a land he knew well where he could turn the very climate and elements against his enemies. In any contest with the Mexicans or the United States army the advantage was always with the Apaches. Knowing the country, they would try to pick the battle site that best suited them, often either a deep canyon or a rocky pass. They seldom attacked unless they thought they were sure to win. They rarely engaged in open combat, relying on ambush or surprise rather than on force of numbers, which the Apaches seldom had. They rarely attacked at night, preferring the early morning. Nor, if they could get out of it, did Apaches fight on horseback. They generally fought on foot.

One Apache war tactic was to fire the dry grass and brush, creating a massive smoke cloud to screen their movements. They had, of course, been using smoke signals for long-distance communication since the sixteenth century.

The Apaches were adept hit-and-run fighters. They struck, killed and burned and looted, and slipped swiftly and silently away like so many ghosts into the desert high country's cacti and rocks. Their losses were light; the damage they left behind was great. If they were closely pursued by superior forces, they scattered in a dozen different directions like a flock of quail, leaving little or no trail to follow. Perhaps hours or even days later they would gather again at a predetermined spot 50 to 100 miles away. And they always had selected an alternative rendevous point in case the first was occupied by an enemy force or was otherwise unsuitable.

Such tactics caused many writers to describe the Apaches as

Western Apache hide war shield decorated with painted ceremonial designs and fringed with eagle feathers.

WESTERN WAYS PHOTO BY CHARLES W. HERBERT

treacherous and cowardly. This is far from the truth. The Apaches firmly believed it wiser to strike and run and live to fight another day. They saw no reason to sacrifice lives needlessly. This practice of avoiding open conflict when they were badly outnumbered or when the terrain was against them postponed their eventual defeat for many years.

By and large the Apaches suffered far fewer casualties than did their enemies. More Spaniards, Mexicans, and Americans lost their lives from Apache attacks during the seventeenth, eighteenth, and nineteenth centuries than did the Apaches. Yet the losses the Apaches suffered, particularly the Chiricahua and Warm Springs Apaches, could not be borne indefinitely by such small tribes. By 1886, when the last of the Chiricahua and Warm Springs Apaches were finally rounded up and shipped off to Florida, their numbers had been cut by two-thirds.

In spite of this lack of numbers, the Apaches were unequalled in fighting efficiency. They possessed cunning, ferocity, endurance, daring, and pure, unadulterated gall. In the opinion of numerous army officers who fought against them, the Chiricahua and Warm Springs and Western Apaches, of all the American Indians, were the greatest all-around fighters.

Unlike so many other Indian tribes the Apaches seldom took scalps. Apaches didn't like to have things belonging to the dead, and neither did Navajos. They believed enemy scalps were magically dangerous and contaminating. An Apache didn't have to bring a scalp home to show what a brave warrior he was. The mere fact that he got back in one piece and with booty proved that. Scalping was, therefore, never carried on extensively. It seems to have been a recently acquired custom. The Chiricahuas blamed the Mexicans for the introduction of scalping, and most scalping seems to have been in retaliation against Spaniards or Mexicans or, later, Americans who had taken Apache scalps.

That doesn't mean that Apaches didn't torture their captives. Sometimes they did, horribly. A victim might be hung head down over a slow fire and roasted. Or he might be tied to a wagon wheel and burned alive, often being skinned in the process. Sometimes Apaches staked a victim naked over an anthill, first smearing the eyes and mouth with wild honey. Again the victim might be bound tightly with green rawhide cords to a giant cactus and left to die as the rawhide tightened as it dried in the sun and the sharp-pointed cactus thorns pierced the victim's body. Similar rawhide thongs might be tied around a captive's head and left to crush the skull as the leather slowly tightened. More than one Mexican rancher was pinned to the ground by a huge stake driven through his body. A number of grave markers in the Fort Bowie cemetery bore the inscription, "Tortured and killed by Apaches." It should be noted, however, that most victims so tortured were individuals who had injured or killed Apaches.

Not all captives were tortured and killed. Occasionally women would be captured, brought back to camp, and put to work as slaves. But the most sought-after captives were young boys of four, five, and six years, who were adopted and brought up as Apaches, some of them frequently rising to high positions within the group.

The Apaches were a match for the best troops sent against them. They were not conquered. They were overpowered by great numbers, by superior equipment, and, above all, by the use of their own Apache brothers against them as scouts.

The Apache Indians
in the
Twentieth Century

TODAY, in the last quarter of the twentieth century, parts of the Southwest are almost as wild and empty as they were a hundred years ago. Today you won't get ambushed at the pass by hostile Apache Indians, but this is still Apache land. There are still plenty of Apaches and Navajos and other Indians in Arizona and New Mexico and the rest of the Southwest; more, in fact, than you will find anyplace else in the United States.

For the Apache Indians are far from vanishing. A century ago there were probably not more than 20,000 Navajos and Apaches in the entire Southwest. Today there are over 8 times that number. The Navajos have actually become the largest single Indian tribe in the United States and Canada, with a population exceeding 146,000. The rest of the Southern Athabascans haven't done quite that well. Yet some 11,000 Western Apaches, 2,000 Jicarillas, and over 1,500 Mescaleros, plus a few hundred Chiricahuas and Warm Springs, Lipans, and Kiowa-Apaches still live in this area.

Except for the Chiricahuas, Warm Springs, and Lipans, the rest of the Apaches and Navajos still live more or less in their original homelands. Yet in most cases these homelands are much smaller than they were a century or two ago. Reservations belonged to the

Indians only until such times as greedy and influential white men wanted a part of them.

No other section of the United States has so many Indians who continue to speak their own language and pursue many of their old social and religious customs. There are more Indians living in the Southwest now than at any time in history or prehistory. The remarkable factor in the history of Indian affairs in the Southwest has been the long-continued isolation and consequent slow-changing cultural pattern of most Indian groups. Up until the First World War, the majority of southwestern Indians knew no more about the outside world than could be learned secondhand and had borrowed little more from the white invaders than domestic animals, plants, tools, and clothing.

Reservation land was not given to the Indians, as many people seem to think. This was Apache land long before the Americans began moving into the Southwest. It still belongs to the Apaches and Navajos. It is owned by the tribal members and is held in trust for them by the United States government. Some tribes have even won lawsuits against the federal government for lands erroneously taken away from them and have received judgment money in payment for the land.

Reservations are not concentration camps; Indians are free to come and go as they please. In theory each Apache or Apache family can choose whether or not to live on his reservation or to continue as a member of his tribe. Actually the choice is not a free one since many reservation Indians depend upon their land and other holdings for a livelihood and, when living on their reservation land, must depend upon membership in the tribe for services not otherwise available. Yet thousands of Apaches and Navajos both live and work in cities and towns outside their reservation boundaries.

The special status of Indians is based on their membership in a tribe and on the fact that, because of this membership, they are a concern of the federal rather than the state government. Such special services as the Indian receives—free schooling, health care, credit financing, and the like—are tied to treaties and to legal and moral obligations of the federal government and are in recognition of the special needs of the Indians.

Like most other people, Apaches must earn their own living. Some do not or can not, like the elderly, the blind, or other needy individuals, and they receive public assistance as do needy members of other groups. An Apache is favored with no dole, no ration, no stipend simply because he is an Indian. He is not a ward or stepchild dependent on a benevolent Great White Father.

All Indians born in the United States are now citizens of the United States and of the states where they live. As citizens of the nation and state, they are subject to all the usual privileges and obligations. An Indian pays sales and gasoline taxes, income and personal property taxes, and other taxes unless exempt by a treaty or another agreement. Since 1924, he has been able to vote, if he can read and write. However, neither Arizona nor New Mexico permitted Indians living on reservations in those states to vote until 1948.

But all of this didn't happen overnight. For nearly half a century after Geronimo's surrender in 1886, the Apaches weren't much better off than they had been. Indian agents continued to come and go. Some were good, some bad. Government policies toward the Indians changed from one administration to another. Under some the Apaches gained a little; under others they lost a little, in some cases even losing more of their lands.

The town of Globe, Arizona, is an example. This area was originally a part of the San Carlos Apache agency. In 1876 a globe-shaped boulder of nearly pure silver was reputedly discovered in rich veins of silver. Miners immediately began pouring into the country, and it wasn't long before this strip of land was taken away from the reservation and opened to mining and settlement. This happened not once but half a dozen times during the next quarter of a century.

With raiding now prohibited and hunting restricted, most Apaches and Navajos managed to eke out a living by using the meager rations they were given, by farming wherever possible, by collecting wild plant foods as they had been doing for centuries, and by sheep and cattle raising.

During this period the Navajos probably fared better than the rest of the Apache groups. They became shepherds and part-time farmers of small patches of corn and melons, scattering out widely with their flocks and even expanding into new territory. As their numbers increased—both in people and in sheep—the government gradually added more and more land to the reservation. Eventually it became the largest Indian reservation in the United States, a vast domain covering 25,000 square miles in northeastern Arizona and northwestern New Mexico and extending slightly into southern Utah and Colorado, an area bigger than some states.

The other Apache groups didn't make out quite as well. The Jicarillas also became shepherds, but on a much smaller scale than the Navajos, although they did gain more land in 1908. They had been farmers for generations and continued to farm after they were placed on the reservation. Only a few Mescaleros had ever been farmers, and most of them still didn't want to become farmers, particularly not under government pressure. They tried sheep and goat raising along with cattle. But like most Apaches, the Mescaleros looked on a horse as a valuable piece of property, a means of prestige and transportation, while a cow was just so much meat on the hoof to be gambled away or immediately eaten. After 1891, with the passage of an act which permitted whites to lease Indian grazing lands, usually cheaply, those Mescaleros who tried to raise cattle found themselves up against stiff competition from neighboring ranchers who had leased the best grazing lands.

Western Apaches faced the same problem. While many Western Apaches had been and still were farmers, much of their two reservations was cattle country. A few Indians had begun to raise cattle in the late 1880s by drawing live cattle in the weekly beef ration and saving them to build up small herds. But beginning in the 1890s invading Anglo-American cattle ranchers soon took over the best-watered Indian lands. By 1920 about five-eighths of the San Carlos reservation alone was under lease to white ranchers, and, through the illegal introduction of thousands of head of unregistered cattle, it was being seriously overgrazed.

Because Indians were herded onto reservations and often crowded closely together around agency headquarters, health became a major problem. In the early days army and agency physicians provided some medical services to the Indians. But hospitals were slow in coming. The first government Indian hospital wasn't opened on the Navajo reservation until 1908. Yet the death rate remained high on most Indian reservations, particularly from tuberculosis.

Both Apaches and Navajos found it difficult to accept the American school system, which was completely foreign to their way of life. At first most of them opposed the government's educational efforts. They did not want to send their children long distances to Indian boarding schools. Nor did they want their youngsters to go to Indian day schools. Navajos opposed schools of any kind on economic grounds, because schools kept the children away from their daily task of herding sheep. But schools eventually were built, and children were taken away, often forcefully, from their homes. In 1892 the first White Mountain Apache school was opened in a vacant Fort Apache barrack. But it required Indian Service officials and Indian scouts and police to round up thirty Apache boys to persuade them to enroll. Schools were generally small and almost always overcrowded. Discipline in school was often rigidly enforced, even for trivial offenses. In fact, school jails on reservations were not abolished until 1927.

The early arrival of Protestant and Roman Catholic missionaries helped alleviate the lack of school facilities, as denominational schools were opened on several of the reservations. Mission hospitals often filled a greater need than their schools. Episcopalian missionaries began operating a hospital at Fort Defiance years before the government had any hospitals at all on the Navajo reservation.

Anglo-American and Mexican-American traders, too, played their part in aiding the Apaches and Navajos to better their economic status. The influence of traders on the Navajo Indians can hardly be overestimated. They were the bearers of a new way of life, their trading posts stocked with everything from coffee, sugar, and flour to canned peaches, saddles, and pocket knives. Most Navajos' only real contact with white people came through the traders, who became their friends, guides, and teachers. Traders were not only merchants but also bankers and pawnshop operators. Trading posts were community centers, places to meet friends and relatives and exchange news and gossip. A visit to the trading post might take up the entire day with endless dickering, looking over the array of merchandise, and talking. Although

Nearly completed Navajo Indian blanket or rug.

TAD NICHOLS

some traders stayed only long enough to make their fortune, many remained to grow up with the country and with the Navajos. They encouraged Navajo production and developed markets for arts and crafts and wool and other raw products.

Navajo women, for example, had learned the art of weaving from the Pueblo Indians around the beginning of the eighteenth century. By 1800, or perhaps even earlier, they had surpassed their Pueblo teachers and were weaving wool into articles of clothing and blankets not only for themselves but for sale or trade to other Indians and to Spaniards and Mexicans. After the Navajos returned from Fort Sumner in 1868 changes in weaving took place as a result of the introduction of commercial dyes and yarn and commercial clothing and yard goods. By the 1890s increasing tourist demand for rugs rather than blankets caused a decline in quality and in native designs. About 1920, largely owing to the efforts of traders and others concerned with raising the standard of Navajo weaving, there was a revival of old blanket patterns and a return to the use of native dyes and wool.

Navajo Indian silverwork is still another example of the influence of the traders. Navajo silverwork, famous the world over, is usually regarded as an ancient art, yet it is actually one of the most recent, dating back to shortly after the middle of the nineteenth century, when a few Navajo ironworkers learned from Mexican silversmiths how to work with silver. At first the Indians used silver quarters, half-dollars, and dollars to fashion into silver bells, headstalls for horses, bowguards, buttons, bracelets, necklaces, belt buckles, and the like, decorated only with simple incised or stamped designs. Silver bells made from quarters were often called mother-in-law bells because women sometimes wore them to give warning to their sons-in-law so that the latter could avoid meeting them face-to-face.

Not until 1880 did the Navajo silversmiths begin to use turquoise for settings in silver jewelry. For centuries southwestern Indians have favored this blue green gem stone for ornaments and offerings. Turquoise was, however, costly. Through the efforts of alert traders and other potential customers new mines were opened in Nevada and Colorado, greatly reducing the price of the precious stones. About 1890, United States authorities finally began enforc-

Navajo silver "squash-blossom" necklace.
TAD NICHOLS

ing already existing laws against defacing United States coins. Traders immediately filled the gap by importing large amounts of Mexican pesos and other coins which were higher in silver content and easier to work.

In many ways the Apaches and Navajos were better off by the early 1930s than they had been at any time during the previous half-century of reservation life, but in other ways they were not. Life was still hard for most of them. Plagued with debt, disease, poverty, and inadequate housing, many of them were discouraged, hopeless, seeing no sure road out of their difficulties.

But a new day was finally dawning for the Indians. In 1934 the United States Congress passed the Indian Reorganization Act which permitted Indians to draw up formal constitutions and govern themselves through elected tribal councils and officers. This was a revolution in bureaucratic thinking: Indian heritage was to be preserved; their arts and crafts were to be encouraged; their religion was not to be interfered with; a fund was set up from which the newly formed tribal governments could borrow money for tribal enterprises. Moreover, this was a voluntary program. In fact, some seventy-three tribes, including the Navajo, originally voted to reject the Act.

The Mescalero Apaches were one of the first tribes to see the advantages of the new program and voted to go along with it in 1936. That same year the San Carlos Apaches also organized reservationwide self-government. By 1938 the Jicarilla Apaches, the White Mountain Apaches, and even the Navajos had set up local tribal councils under the Reorganization Act. Each tribal council, usually elected every two to four years, administers the affairs of the entire tribe, including the management of all tribal property and tribal enterprises, control of both Indians and non-Indians on the reservation, and the welfare of tribal members.

For peoples who had never before been organized on a tribal basis, this was a drastic step to take. Most of the Apaches had never thought of themselves as tribes. The Western Apaches, for instance, originally included at least five more or less distinct groups—White Mountain, Cibecue, San Carlos, Southern Tonto, and Northern Tonto—each of which was further divided into from two to four different bands. There was no strong feeling

Western Apache wickiup standing beside a government-built house, the latter being used as a storeroom while the Apache family lives in the wickiup.

TAD NICHOLS

of unity, no organized leadership for even an entire band, let alone an entire group. Now all of these, plus members of some of the other Apache groups, found themselves divided and organized into two tribes, the White Mountain Apache Tribe on the Fort Apache Indian Reservation and the San Carlos Apache Tribe on the San Carlos Reservation. Similarly, on the Mescalero Indian Reservation in New Mexico there were Mescaleros, Chiricahuas, Warm Springs and Mimbres Apaches, and a few Lipan Apaches, all now bound together as the Mescalero Apache Tribe.

Although there have been many problems and difficulties to overcome, so far the tribal government system seems to be working out extremely well. Both Apaches and Navajos take a lively interest in council affairs, and council meetings are always well attended. Election races for council seats are hotly contested, and voting is generally heavy. For those who couldn't read, the Navajo Tribal Council originally used colored ribbons to identify candidates but in 1950 replaced the ribbons with pictorial paper ballots. Women take an active part in elections and have been elected to councils.

As one San Carlos tribal official told the writer, the Apaches are participating fully in their own government, and United States citizens outside the reservation could well follow the example of strong interest shown by the Indians in their local governments.

With the establishment of reservationwide tribal government, changes weren't long in coming to the Apache way of life. Indian leaders recognized that their youngsters had to learn English, reading, writing, and such other subjects as mathematics if they were to live happily and successfully in the modern world. One of the first things the White Mountain tribal council did was to make school attendance compulsory for children between the ages of six and eighteen, with school bus drivers serving as truant officers. The San Carlos tribal council enacted a similar amendment to their tribal laws. Juvenile officers check every school bus and investigate each child absent from school, taking legal action against the parents when a child is absent without good cause. In time the White Mountain Apache tribe, along with most other Apache tribes, began providing college scholarships for worthy high school graduates.

The Bureau of Indian Affairs also began stepping up its efforts to aid Apache and Navajo education. Its educational program was reorganized to include adult training and to make school buildings community centers. The government greatly expanded its primary school program for the Navajos, even opening small schools in remote corners of the reservation.

During this era of reformation in Indian policies and later, the Bureau of Indian Affairs built new agency headquarters on the various Apache and Navajo reservations. On the Navajo reservation they consolidated their six widely separated agencies into a single agency in a new administrative town in northeastern Arizona, called Window Rock after a nearby natural red rock formation. Here there is also a hogan-styled octagonal stone building large enough to house the seventy-four members of the Navajo Tribal Council. Smaller Navajo council houses have been built all across the reservation where leaders can meet and rule on local affairs. Window Rock is often referred to as the Navajo Indian capital. Here in recent years a Navajo radio station has been sending news and bulletins in both Navajo and English to members of the tribe all over the reservation.

San Carlos is the headquarters for the Bureau of Indian Affairs on the San Carlos Indian reservation and also for the San Carlos Tribal administrative and business offices. Fort Apache on the Fort Apache Indian reservation was manned by the United States Cavalry until 1924, when it was turned over to the Indian Service for use as a school. The town of Whiteriver, four miles up the North Fork of White River from Fort Apache, is now the administrative heart of the reservation and includes the Bureau of Indian Affairs offices, the White Mountain Tribal Council headquarters and offices, and a community building.

In New Mexico the town of Mescalero is headquarters for the offices of both the Mescalero Tribal Council and the Bureau of Indian Affairs, with the town of Dulce playing a similar role on the Jicarilla Apache reservation in the extreme northern part of the state.

While most Bureau of Indian Affairs agencies were originally almost entirely staffed with Anglo-Americans or Mexican-Americans, the majority of government employees are now Indians, furnishing employment for hundreds of Apaches and Navajos. In 1971 a Navajo Indian, Anthony Lincoln, became the first Navajo Area Director in the Bureau of Indian Affairs office at Window Rock.

During the 1930s, two newly formed government agencies, the Soil Conservation Service and the Civilian Conservation Corps, with separate branches for the Indians, helped both Apaches and Navajos with land management problems and other conservation measures on the various reservations. The Bureau of Indian Affairs, with funding aid through the Indian division of the Civilian Conservation Corps, initiated large-scale range improvement projects, road construction, and other work programs among the Navajos.

Perhaps the biggest revolution due to tribal self-government came in business enterprises. With the closing of the last of the outside cattle leases in the early 1930s and with the encouragement of the tribal council the Western Apaches went into the cattle business in a big way. Over the years the Apaches have become as excellent top cowhands and cattle raisers as their grandfathers had been cattle rustlers and raiders and fighters.

The San Carlos tribe has its own registered tribal herd of pure-bred Hereford cattle and also operates a tribal stock enterprise (the "old folks" herd) to support a tribal welfare program, its own form of social security for the aged. The White Mountain tribe has its own tribal herd of registered Herefords.

These tribal herds occupy only a small percentage of the reservation lands, and most of the grazing areas are used by a number of cattle associations run by the Apaches themselves. All Apache cattlemen belong to one or the other of these associations and run their stock on association range. The association, through payments in labor or fees from members, maintains and works the range. Cattle are, however, individually owned and branded. There are now over 1,200 individual Apache cattlemen owning from a few head each up to the limit of 70 breeding cows.

In more recent years an even more profitable business enterprise for the White Mountain Apaches has been the sale of standing timber to commercial operators. In addition, they have more than doubled their tribal income from their timber resources by building and operating their own sawmills at Whiteriver, at the same time providing jobs for several hundred Apaches. The San Carlos Apaches, too, receive considerable royalties from the sale of timber.

Both the San Carlos and White Mountain tribes also operate trading enterprises and have encouraged and helped finance Apaches to start up private businesses such as service stations, garages, stores, restaurants, and motels. The San Carlos Apaches have a tribal farm of several hundred acres and raise alfalfa, grain, and cotton. Future plans call for a considerable expansion in their farm acreage.

Another recent profitable Apache industry has been the mining and sale of peridot, one of the world's oldest yet least-known gem stones, which is formed by the fires of a volcano. One of the very few places in the world where this greenish colored peridot occurs is in an extensive lava formation known as Peridot Mesa on the San Carlos Indian reservation. Free-lance Apache diggers collect the rough gem stones and sell them to two major markets, one of which is nonreservation processors. The other is the Peridot Mining and Marketing Project, a government-sponsored Apache company, already self-sustaining, that cuts, polishes, finishes, and then wholesales thousands of dollars worth of all types of Indian jewelry every month.

A still more recent San Carlos Apache business venture is concerned with the seeds of the wild jojoba (pronounced ho-ho-bah) plant, a desert shrub indigenous to parts of southern Arizona and California and northern Mexico and particularly abundant on the San Carlos reservation. According to scientific studies, more than half of the peanut-sized jojoba seed is an oil which is resistant to high temperatures and pressures, making it an ideal substitute for the sperm whale oil widely used for lubricating machinery. The supply of the latter oil is becoming extremely limited, as this whale has been placed on the endangered species list, and the United States has barred further imports of the oil. The University of Arizona and other laboratories have discovered that jojoba oil has many other potential uses—cosmetics, self-polishing wax, detergents, wax coatings for paper, paint remover, ornaments, high-protein animal food supplements, and possibly in medicine. For these reasons jojoba oil has often been called "liquid gold."

In 1972 under the supervision of University of Arizona researchers, the San Carlos Apaches collected more than 87,000 pounds of jojoba seeds. But the scientists concluded that the wild plant would have to be cultivated on a large scale before jojoba oil could become an economically profitable industry. In 1974 the San Carlos tribe received a $145,000 grant from the Department of Health, Education, and Welfare and incorporated the Apache Marketing Cooperative Association to develop a jojoba tribal industry. It is already marketing hand-dipped candles made of jojoba wax from wild plants harvested on the reservation. These are high-quality candles that are clean burning and almost dripless. However, its major project has been the clearing and planting of several thousand jojoba seedlings on the reservation, a beginning that may become a new industry for the tribe.

The Mescalero Apaches also operate a number of tribal business enterprises. Besides individually owned herds of cattle, there is a tribal herd and a herd belonging to the Cattle Growers Association. Timber is, however, a more important tribal resource than cattle. Trees are scientifically harvested by lumber companies under the supervision of a forester. Other tribal industries include a tribal store, a woodyard for firewood for reservation use and for sale to neighboring towns, a tribal crew cutting small trees for the Christmas tree market, and tribal crews maintaining dams, ditches, corrals, and roads.

"Join the Red Hats and see the world!" That is the slogan of the famous Red Hats, teams of volunteer airborne Indian fire fighters formed in 1948 by the Mescalero Apaches in cooperation with the United States Forest Service. Wearing a distinctive red striped steel helmet, the Mescalero fire fighters have since been joined by other teams of Navajo and Pueblo Indians. These Red Hats have become highly efficient fire fighters. A twenty-four-person squad of Red Hats can build a fire trail as fast as a person can walk. During the fire season they are kept busy all over the West.

While the Jicarilla Apaches have several thousand head of cattle and innumerable horses, most of them derive their income from sheep raising. But the tribe's biggest sources of revenue are leases for hundreds of producing gas and oil wells on their reservation lands and the sale of timber.

Half a century ago most Anglo-Americans would have agreed that the Navajo reservation, vast as it was, was largely sand and rocks and not fit for much more than raising sheep and jackrabbits. It was just that then, but today the Navajo tribe is engaged in big business running far up into the millions of dollars and requiring the services of a large staff of skilled attorneys, accountants, auditors, insurance agents, realtors, and a budget bureau. For this high semidesert Navajo country contains vast natural resources—huge deposits of coal, oil, natural gas, helium, vanadium, uranium, timber, sand, and gravel. Various corporate enterprises paid the Navajo tribe extremely well for the privilege of exploiting these newly discovered natural resources. Wise Navajo leaders insisted that employment preference be given to Navajos whenever possible, thus adding many new jobs to the reservation payroll. The Navajo tribe operates its own utility companies, including a multimillion dollar steam generating plant fueled by reservation-mined coal, and supplies electricity, gas, and fuel to the Navajos for both domestic and industrial uses.

The Navajo Tribal Council built a new lumber mill employing nearly 500 Navajos in the high pine country along the Arizona-New Mexico border. They also financed numerous Navajo small businesses, including a coal mine, a wool processing plant, an arts and crafts guild, and several motels.

Over the years Navajos and Apaches have become skilled technicians and wage earners, working as mechanics, machine operators, plumbers, electricians, carpenters, nurses, clerks, and laborers both on and off their reservations. This was due in large part to the wholesale displacement of individuals and families during and immediately after the Second World War. Thousands of Apaches and Navajos served in the armed forces, where they quickly proved that they hadn't lost the fighting abilities of their ancestors. Many Navajos volunteered long before they were drafted; even old men carrying ancient guns showed up at the registration boards and asked where they could find the enemy.

Some Navajo men performed a unique and valuable service to the war effort. When the Japanese began cracking United States army codes, the signal corps called in teams of Navajo Indians to transmit by portable telephone or two-way radios vital messages in Navajo. That provided an absolutely unbreakable code, as Navajo was one language no Japanese had ever learned. Neither was the Apache language, and a number of Apaches also served as code talkers.

Thousands of other Indians, many taking their families with them, left their reservations for California and elsewhere throughout the West to take full- or part-time jobs in war industries or in harvesting wartime crops. While this brought prosperity to many Navajos and Apaches, usually for the first time, their new experiences outside the reservation made them realize the handicaps under which they had been living. Their first long look at the outside world brought an awareness of white people's ways and the values of formal education, modern medicine, and the American economic system. Returning soldiers and war workers brought back to their reservations new desires for money, more adequate housing and other facilities, more possessions, and better education. While changes did come in these areas, they took time. One of the first sources for new tribal revenue to help finance such enterprises came in the blossoming tourist trade following the war.

Less than a century after fighting to keep any and all intruders —Spaniards, Mexicans, and Americans—out of their homelands, the Apaches and Navajos are now welcoming their former enemies with open arms. For the Indians have learned that one of the greatest assets of their reservations is recreation—hunting, fishing, boating, swimming, skiing, hiking, or just plain sightseeing. In addition, they have realized that their ancient culture and traditional ways of life present a unique attraction to modern people. They have also discovered that tourists can and do bring sorely needed cash to the reservations.

The White Mountain Apaches were among the first to take advantage of their natural paradise of mountains, streams, lakes, and forests. In 1954 the tribal council established the White Mountain Recreational Enterprise to develop their high country land into a playground for tourists, hunters, and fishermen.

One of their first projects ran into trouble. They planned to build a dam and create an artificial lake on one of the small upper tributaries of the Salt River. The Salt River Valley Water Users' Association immediately took legal action to prevent damming the stream and storing water which, rightfully, they said, belonged to them. Over the years this Phoenix organization had claimed rights to water on even the smallest Salt River tributary. They got an injunction against construction and forced the construction company work crews off the damsite. But the Apaches thought that if anyone could claim water flowing on their own reservation, it was the Apaches, not some outside organization hundreds of miles away. Quietly they hired independent operators and went on with the work. Papers were drawn up ordering them to stop all work on the dam and were given to the sheriff to serve. But the Apaches hadn't forgotten the tactics of their ancestors. Blocking all roads to the site with bulldozers, they stationed armed guards all around the area and informed state law enforcement officers that only Indian tribal police or United States marshals could serve papers on the reservation. Working around the clock, construction crews completed the dam in ten days, naming the newly created reservoir Hawley Lake after their reservation superintendent. Legal action continued in the courts for another decade before the suit against the Apaches was finally dismissed in 1966.

But the Apaches didn't wait for the courts to settle the issue. During that decade they built twenty-six more recreational lakes. With the construction of new fish hatcheries on the reservation, a steady supply of hundreds of thousands of trout and other game fish was insured for stocking these and other lakes and streams. In addition, the Apaches have developed hundreds of new campgrounds; improved existing roads and trails and built hundreds of miles of new ones; constructed motels, cottages, and lodges around reservation lakes and streams; laid water mains; installed power lines; built ski resorts, lodges, and ski lifts, with facilities for ice fishing and snowmobiling, boat docks, trailer parks, stores, service stations, and restaurants; and leased over a thousand cabin sites around Hawley and other lakes. Through the sale of reservation camping, fishing, and hunting permits, they have added thousands of dollars to tribal revenues. They have encouraged the manufacture of native arts and crafts, particularly various types of twined-woven and coiled basketry, cradleboards, and beadwork for sale through tribal stores. In fact, the White Mountain Apache Recreational Enterprise has been so successful that its program has become a model for other Indian tribes.

There is much history surrounding old Fort Apache, originally established in 1870 high on lava bluffs at the junction of the east and north forks of White River. Officers' row and the old post headquarters building are still in use, and General Crook's log cabin still stands. Cochise visited here, and many famous Apache scouts trained here. Troops and scouts from Fort Apache pursued Geronimo and Nachez and other Apache leaders. To preserve some of their own cultural heritage, the Apache Tribal Council maintains a culture center in an old Fort Apache log cabin dating back to 1875. Up the hill from the fort is the military cemetery marking the resting place of Apache scouts and their families. You can still see the deep wagon ruts marking the old military road from Fort Apache to Fort Thomas.

Monument Valley in northeastern Arizona and southeastern Utah.

The San Carlos Apaches have also begun developing the heavily forested and mountainous northern and eastern parts of their reservation as recreational areas. They have improved roads, put in a number of lakes stocked with game fish, and built campgrounds, cabins, and stores. They have recently taken over the operation of new recreational facilities at San Carlos Reservoir in the southern part of the reservation, including a boat dock, campgrounds, picnic areas, a store, and a restaurant.

The San Carlos Apaches hold the distinction of being the first tribe in the Southwest, if not in the nation, to hold membership in a chamber of commerce. On September 24, 1952, the San Carlos Apache tribe joined the Safford, Arizona, Chamber of Commerce.

Like the Western Apaches, the Mescalero Apaches have gone into the recreation business. They have opened a tourist center at Apache Summit on the main highway through the scenic Sacramento Mountains, built a ski lift and resort, and are encouraging the manufacture and sale of native arts and crafts, including baskets, dresses, and moccasins. In 1975 they built a 22-million-dollar,

134-room deluxe resort, the Inn of the Mountain Gods, complete with an artificial lake, swimming pools, tennis courts, and a golf course.

One of the major Jicarilla Apache tribal recreational enterprises centers on Dulce Lake, where the Indians have built a motel, stores, and other facilities for tourists. Small lakes and streams in their high pine country attract many hunters and fishermen.

The Navajos have been particularly active in encouraging tourists to visit their once secluded reservation. Recognizing the importance of their spectacular scenic wonders, ranging from magnificent Monument Valley and the Grand Canyon to Canyon de Chelly, Lake Powell, and the Painted Desert, they have set aside half a dozen of the most colorful of these as tribal parks, each complete with tourist information centers, camping grounds, and picnic sites. To make them more easily accessible, they have constructed hundreds of miles of paved roads and improved still more. They have organized a large staff of Navajo park rangers with radio-equipped trucks to serve and assist visitors. Through the tribal council the Navajos have built their own motels, service stations, garages, restaurants, and even their own trading posts.

The Navajo tribal government is trying to insure that their proud heritage is not soon forgotten. In 1961 they established the Navajo Tribal Museum at Window Rock to preserve the culture and history not only of the Navajo themselves but also of other historic and prehistoric southwestern Indian tribes in that area. In its collections are oustanding displays of Navajo blankets and rugs, silver and turquoise jewelry, and other native arts and crafts, as well as exhibits illustrating the geology, paleontology, fauna, and flora of the region. Next to the museum is the tribal zoo. Historic and prehistoric sites on the reservation are being preserved for visitors, and tribal arts and crafts can also be seen at special centers.

In 1960 the Navajos began publishing their own newspaper, the *Navajo Times*, a project of their Public Relations and Information Department. Published at Window Rock, this illustrated weekly newspaper contains much information about the arts and crafts and history of the Navajos and about places of interest to visit on the reservation.

To prepare their children for work both on and off the reservation, the Navajo Tribal Council has set up a 10-million-dollar fund to provide college scholarships, particularly for young men and women who wish to train for professions.

The year 1969 marked another outstanding educational advance for the Navajos, the opening of a Navajo community college, the first institution of higher learning to be established and controlled by an Indian tribe. Its modern campus, built with tribal, federal, foundation, and individually contributed funds, sprawls over a 2,000-acre site about 40 miles north of Window Rock. The college will specialize in vocational training in traditional Navajo handicrafts, in Navajo culture, in administrative and tribal management, and in remedial adult courses and other community-oriented programs. A branch college has opened at Shiprock, New Mexico, and already has several hundred students.

The Navajos have recently begun operating their own Navajo airline. The half-dozen small planes of this new airline will be used to give the Navajos better health care and general charter service. In addition to flights within the 25,000-square-mile reservation, the airline will run charter flights carrying Navajos to and from Phoenix, Albuquerque, and Farmington. Present plans call for building at least five paved landing fields and from thirty to thirty-five graded airstrips on the reservation.

Housing for Indians on most reservations has generally lagged far behind other projects. When new houses were built, they were usually located in and around such already established settlements as Whiteriver, San Carlos, Bylas, Mescalero, Dulce, Window Rock, Fort Defiance, Shiprock, or Tuba City. Although these houses helped those working in or near these towns, the policy tended to concentrate the Indians in certain areas even more compactly than they had ever been. On the Mescalero reservation, for example, over a third of the Indians live in or around the town of Mescalero. The situation is the same on the San Carlos reservation, with well over half the total population living at or near the agency town of San Carlos and most of the remaining Apaches at the towns of Bylas and Calva. This was, of course, completely foreign to the old Apache and Navajo pattern of small, widely scattered family, joint family, or local group communities.

Conditions are somewhat different on both the Fort Apache and

Navajo reservations. Although Whiteriver is the tribal and trading center to the White Mountain Apaches, there are other communities up and down White River and on Cibecue and Carrizo and Cedar Creeks. Large numbers of Navajos may be concentrated at Window Rock and half a dozen other large towns, but small settlements can be found all over the huge Navajo reservation.

However, with more and more Apaches and Navajos turning to wage labor, either for industry, the tribe, or the government, housing must be provided where the jobs are in the towns. In 1971 the first project approved by the Federal Housing Administration on an Arizona Indian reservation provided for building 186 units at Fort Defiance on the Navajo reservation. Later that same year a second and even larger federally funded Navajo housing development was begun at Shiprock, New Mexico, for 214 single-family dwellings and 41 apartments. In that same year planners for the Navajo Housing Authority were designing 700 low-rent, 3- to 5-bedroom housing units to be erected at 35 different locations on the reservation. White Mountain Apaches are also beginning to participate in a mutual help housing program for their reservation.

Unlike most other southwestern Indians, neither the Apaches nor the Navajos have a regular calendar of ceremonies. The White Mountain Apaches have, however, adopted two of our holidays to celebrate, the Fourth of July and Labor Day. Generally they schedule a girls' puberty ceremony at Whiteriver to coincide with the Fourth of July, with the traditional masked Gan dancers performing nightly. That event also calls for a rodeo, baseball and other games, nightly social dances, and feasting. The Mescalero Apaches usually hold their ceremony for girls on July 1.

The White Mountain Apaches celebrate Labor Day as an occasion for an annual tribal fair and rodeo at Whiteriver. Schools, missions, and federal agencies set up exhibits, and there are highly decorated booths containing displays of everything from garden crops to Apache costumes and craft products. In addition to the rodeo there are baseball games, a fried-bread-making contest, and evening Indian dances.

The Navajos have numerous curing and other ceremonies taking place at almost any time during the year. Today some of these, such as the so-called Squaw Dance, are so popular that white

Navajo girl, arrayed in her best costume and finest jewelry, waiting for the Squaw Dance during an Enemy Way curing chant.

TAD NICHOLS

people often take part in them. Each year in August the Navajo Intertribal Ceremonial brings together more than thirty different Indian tribes at Gallup, New Mexico, where thousands of visitors witness Indian dances performed by the various tribes, a rodeo, wagon and horse races, barbecues, and craft displays.

The Apache way of life has changed in the past 100 years of reservation life. Warfare and raiding have gone. The old local Apache group headed by a chief has been largely replaced by an elected tribal council. Law is now enforced by Indian police and Indian courts under the direction of the tribal government, except for major crimes, which come under federal jurisdiction. Cattle raising or employment outside the reservation has become the Apache's principal occupation, with sheep taking their place on the Navajo reservation. The plow is now used in farming, as are other mechanical conveniences. A pickup truck has replaced the foot and the horse as the favorite means of transportation. Yet the horse is still king on most reservations. Navajos still show up for dances and ceremonials in wagons or on horseback.

Though the long, voluminous bright skirts and high-necked blouses of the late nineteenth century are still popular with many Apache women, the men have generally adopted the typical Western cowboy outfit of tight-fitting shirt, jeans, and boots, with the wide-brimmed Stetson replacing the headband. Both men and women prefer velveteen shirts in solid colors. Most Navajo men and women usually wear ankle-high, hard-soled moccasins of brown leather fastened across the instep with a silver button. Small Apache and Navajo girls, barely able to toddle, are often dressed just like their mothers.

The old staples—wild plants, seeds, fruits, and wild game—are no longer important sources of food, though most Apaches and Navajos still have small patches of corn, peaches, melons, beans, and other garden produce. For Navajos mutton is the chief meat dish, while Apaches prefer beef when they can get it. Like most of us today these Indians are primarily dependent on storebought foods, particularly canned goods, bought at the many trading posts and stores on the reservations. Candy and soda pop are two of the most popular items at any reservation store. Alcoholism is still a serious social problem among both Apaches and Navajos.

Nearly all Apache and Navajo children are now in school, learning white people's languages and ways. But absenteeism is high on many reservations, because some Navajo youngsters ride horseback ten to twenty miles to get to school. Others ride up to sixty miles each way on busses. Yet even though all of the younger generation and nearly all of the middle-aged and older Indians speak English and sometimes Spanish or Mexican as well, English is still not their native language. Some of the older tribesmen still speak no English at all. Native Indian languages are still very much alive and flourishing on practically every Indian reservation in the Southwest. In 1976 two White Mountain Apaches trained in linguistics developed a written form of Apache, with thirty-two consonants and five vowels, as compared to nineteen consonants and seven vowels in English, and are now teaching classes in the language at Fort Apache.

The Apache is still an Apache and will be for a long, long time to come. While it wouldn't be true to say that the Apaches and Navajos are living much as they have always lived, change has come more slowly than it has to most other southwestern Indians not so geographically isolated.

Cochise, Victorio, Nana, Geronimo, and Manuelito have all gone to the Indian Happy Hunting Ground. The word Apache, which once heralded death and destruction to the settlers of Arizona and New Mexico, now stands for a people who are attempting to build a place for themselves in the white world and at the same time retain something of their native culture. Prospects are even brighter for that. In October 1973 the seven Apache Indian tribes in Arizona and New Mexico announced the formation of the Apache Nations Alliance. The member tribes of this new alliance agreed to help and support each other in fighting poverty and gaining better education, health services, housing, and employment opportunities on their reservations. The tribes also agreed to support efforts to perpetuate Apache culture and to protect their natural resources.

Many customs still survive from the past. Family and other kinship ties are still strong and so too is the mother-in-law taboo. Descent is still reckoned in the matrilineal line. Marriage procedure has not greatly changed; many marriages are still arranged by the two families rather than by the individuals themselves. Marriage gifts are still given, usually ranging from a steer or sheep killed for the woman's family to a load of supplies from the trading post or, in at least one case, to a gift of seventy-five dollars by the young man to his future mother-in-law. Today, in addition, a marriage license and ceremony according to state laws are required. Modern divorce differs from the old pattern only in that the government requires that the separation be legalized in court.

The traditional hogan is still home for a great many Navajo families, particularly for those still herding sheep and goats away from the towns. Many of these well-built log or rock hogans have electricity and television. Pole and brush wickiups, now covered with canvas rather than with skins, can still be seen on the Apache reservations. Many women still prefer to cook over an open fire. Except for most of the utensils used, methods of preparing food are much the same as they were a hundred years ago.

While you may not recognize an Apache or Navajo medicine man or witch or magician, they are still there and still operating much as they always have. In spite of four centuries of Spanish, Mexican, and American efforts to suppress or stamp out native Indian religion, old ideas of the supernatural still persist. In fact, only within the past fifty years has the United States government officially stopped interference with Indian ceremonial and religious life. The fact that magic, witchcraft, and medicine men are still very much alive in the Southwest is evidenced in the following twentieth-century true stories.

They say lightning never strikes twice in the same place, but it did in Tucson, Arizona, in August 1955. Within a period of ten days lightning twice blasted a tall palm tree standing near several houses and cabins. These houses and surrounding cabins were part of a United States government rest home for tubercular Navajo Indians. Like the hooting of an owl, lightning is a Navajo omen of illness and danger. To Navajos already sick, lightning might be doubly potent. At least this seems to have been the thought of most of the seventy-odd Navajo patients after the second bolt of lightning struck the same palm tree. Two Navajo women immediately left for the reservation, and others began packing their belongings to follow them. To calm the uneasy patients a medicine

A twentieth-century Navajo medicine man. TAD NICHOLS

man was flown down from the Navajo reservation. After chanting one of the curing chants over the hospital's communication system, the medicine man dipped a feathered prayer stick into a basket of sacred herbal medicine and sprinkled drops of the medicine on the lightning-struck palm tree, on the ground around it, on the houses, and on each of the patients. This curing ceremony evidently chased away whatever evil spirits were causing the trouble, and the patients unpacked their bags and were soon back at their normal round of activities. The only reminder of the event was one lone, fire-blackened palm tree which was left standing until most of the Navajo patients had returned to the reservation. So far, lightning hasn't struck again.

Nor is this an isolated case. More and more doctors in Navajo hospitals, increasingly aware of how many real ailments from ulcers to loss of speech may be brought on by fear, worry, hysteria, and the like, are allowing medicine men to perform chants by a patient's bedside. This frees the patient of worry and fright caused by the fear of witchcraft or of the anger of ghosts or other evil spirits and gives the doctor's medication a better chance to do its healing work. In many cases those Apaches and Navajos who first go to doctors and do not get immediate relief then go to medicine men.

In December 1970 the chief psychiatrist at a New Mexico hospital was advertising for applicants for a new staff position, that of diviner or medicine man, who could help those Indian patients who believed they were bewitched. According to the report, there were a dozen such patients in the hospital at that time. All that was required to qualify for the job was five years' experience as a diviner.

Navajos and Apaches still take their witchcraft seriously. Accounts of witches and witch killings occasionally make the headlines, like one in New Mexico in 1942, when a Navajo blamed the death of his three children on witchcraft and killed three suspected witches.

In 1973 a new Navajo high school was built with the main entrance facing the wrong direction. Since the Navajos believe that the entrance to a building must always face the east, the direction of all that is good, a medicine man had to be called in to take the

To counteract the effects of evil spirits, a Navajo medicine man sprinkles medicine on a lightning-struck palm tree and on the ground around it.

curse off the school before the Indians would use the building.

Still, changes have taken place in certain native Indian customs and beliefs over the course of the past thirty or forty years. The taboo against eating fish isn't as strong as it used to be. And although Western Apaches still burn the deceased's wickiup and his possessions, if the family is living in a house and someone dies, the family usually just moves out for several months. Formerly an Apache's best horse was killed at the grave so that his spirit would be well mounted on its long journey through shadowland. Since the authorities now frown on this practice, the horse is often taken up into the remote hills and killed. At the burial of an Apache woman, a sewing machine is sometimes placed on her grave, along with a supply of canned goods, a great favorite among the Apaches.

Although strictly traditional burial practices are still followed in remote areas of the Navajo country, Navajos living in larger reservation settlements frequently have church or other public funerals for deceased relatives. In addition, they sometimes bury substantial amounts of money with the deceased instead of items of silver and turquoise jewelry or other valuable personal effects as they used to do.

Navajos and Apaches, along with most other southwestern Indians, have a keen sense of humor. Some of them even joke about death, as witness their story about the Navajo burial attendant who picked up the cash offering in the grave and left his own personal check in its place.

Times may change, yet old beliefs still persist. Four is still the sacred or lucky number for Apaches and Navajos. They still take great care not to offend the rain and water spirits and the winds that blow the clouds, the home of the rain spirits, across their fields. The hooting of an owl still sends chills up the spines of Navajos and Apaches. Witches and sorcerers and ghosts, so the Indians say, still prowl around in the dead of night, and many Apaches and Navajos still carry protection against witches and sorcerers. And throughout it all is still woven the color and pageantry of their ancient tribal rituals and ceremonies.

The average Apache or Navajo, like many of his Indian cousins all over the United States and Canada, is still reluctant to discard the traditions of his ancestors. Today when millions of Americans are dabbling in astrology, fortune-telling, and witchcraft or carrying rabbit's feet for good luck, who are we to say that Apache and Navajo beliefs about omens and sorcery and witches and curing chants are wrong.

We can end this story of the Apache Indians on no more ceremonial a note than to quote the concluding lines common to most Navajo prayers:

> *In beauty I walk.*
> *With beauty before me, may I walk.*
> *With beauty behind me, may I walk.*
> *With beauty above me, may I walk.*
> *With beauty below me, may I walk.*
> *With beauty all around me, may I walk.*
> *It is finished in beauty.*
> *It is finished in beauty.*

As an old Apache might say—Enjuh, all is well.

Bibliography

LITERALLY thousands of books, articles, and reports have been written about the Apache Indians. Merely listing them would fill up this entire volume and several more besides. Unfortunately many of these are highly technical, while others are frequently either out of print or hard to find. The following list of more or less popularly written and generally available books and articles is for the interested reader who wants further information on the Apache Indians.

ADAMS, ALEXANDER B. *Geronimo, a Biography*. New York: G. P. Putnam's Sons, 1971.

AMSDEN, CHARLES A. *Navaho Weaving*. Albuquerque: University of New Mexico Press, 1949.

BAHTI, TOM. *Southwestern Indian Arts and Crafts*. Flagstaff, Ariz.: KC Publications, 1964.

———. *Southwestern Indian Tribes*. Flagstaff, Ariz.: KC Publications, 1968.

BAILEY, L. R. *Indian Slave Trade in the Southwest*. Los Angeles: Westernlore Press, 1966.

———. *The Long Walk*. Los Angeles: Westernlore Press, 1964.

BALDWIN, GORDON C. *How Indians Really Lived*. New York: G. P. Putnam's Sons, 1967.

————. *Indians of the Southwest*. New York: G. P. Putnam's Sons, 1970.

————. *The Warrior Apaches*. Tucson, Ariz.: Dale Stuart King, 1965.

BALL, EVE. *In the Days of Victorio*. Tucson: University of Arizona Press, 1970.

BARRETT, S. M., ed. *Geronimo, His Own Story*. New York: E. P. Dutton & Co., Inc., 1970.

BASSO, KEITH H. *Western Apache Witchcraft*. Tucson: University of Arizona Press, 1969.

BENNETT, KAY. *Kaibah, Recollections of a Navajo Childhood*. Los Angeles: Westernlore Press, 1964.

BETZINEZ, JASON, with W. S. NYE. *I Fought with Geronimo*. Harrisburg, Pa.: The Stackpole Company, 1959.

BIGELOW, JOHN, JR., ed. by ARTHUR WOODWARD. *On the Bloody Trail of Geronimo*. Los Angeles: Westernlore Press, 1958. Paperback edition, Tower Books, New York, 1968.

BOURKE, JOHN G. *An Apache Campaign in the Sierra Madre*. New York: Charles Scribner's Sons, 1958.

————. *On the Border with Crook*. New York: Charles Scribner's Sons, 1891. Reprinted by Long's College Book Company, Columbus, Ohio, 1950.

————. *The Medicine Men of the Apache*. Glorieta, N.M.: Rio Grande Press, 1970.

BRANDES, RAY. *Frontier Military Posts of Arizona*. Globe, Ariz.: Dale Stuart King, 1960.

CASTETTER, EDWARD F., and MORRIS E. OPLER. "The Ethnobiology of the Chiricahua and Mescalero Apache," *University of New Mexico Bulletin*, Biological Series, no. 5, 1936.

CLUM, WOODWORTH. *Apache Agent*. New York: Houghton-Mifflin Company, 1936.

CORBUSIER, W. T. *Verde to San Carlos*. Tucson, Ariz.: Dale Stuart King, 1969.

CREMONY, JOHN C. *Life among the Apaches*. Tucson, Ariz.: Arizona Silhouettes, 1951. Reprinted by Rio Grande Press, Glorieta, N.M., 1969.

CRUSE, THOMAS. *Apache Days and After*. Caldwell, Idaho: The Caxton Printers, Ltd., 1941.

DAVIS, BRITTON. *The Truth about Geronimo*. New Haven, Conn.: Yale University Press, 1929.

DOBYNS, HENRY F. *The Apache People*. Phoenix, Ariz.: Indian Tribal Series, 1971.

DOBYNS, HENRY F., and ROBERT C. EULER. *The Navajo People*. Phoenix, Ariz.: Indian Tribal Series, 1972.

DUTTON, BERTHA P. *Indians of the American Southwest*. Englewood Cliffs, N.J.: Prentice-Hall, 1975.

FORREST, EARLE R. *With a Camera in Old Navaholand*. Norman: University of Oklahoma Press, 1969.

GOODWIN, GRENVILLE. *The Social Organization of the Western Apache*. Chicago: The University of Chicago Press, 1942.

GOODWIN, GRENVILLE, ed. by KEITH H. BASSO. *Western Apache Raiding and Warfare*. Tucson: University of Arizona Press, 1971.

HERBERT, CHARLES W. "Land of the White Mountain Apaches," *Arizona Highways Magazine*, vol. 37, no. 7, pp. 6–39, 1962.

HERBERT, LUCILE and CHARLES W. "Land of the San Carlos Apaches," *Arizona Highways Magazine*, vol. 39, no. 5, pp. 8–35, 1963.

KENT, KATE PECK. *The Story of Navaho Weaving*. Phoenix, Ariz.: The Heard Museum of Anthropology and Primitive Art, 1961.

KLUCKHOHN, CLYDE. *Navaho Witchcraft*. Boston: Beacon Press, paperback edition, 1967.

————, W. W. HILL, and LUCY WALES KLUCKHOHN. *Navaho Material Culture*. Cambridge, Mass.: Belknap Press of Harvard University Press, 1971.

———— and DOROTHEA LEIGHTON. *The Navaho*. New York: Doubleday & Company, Inc., 1962.

LOCKWOOD, FRANK C. *The Apache Indians*. New York: The Macmillan Company, 1938.

MAILS, THOMAS E. *The People Called Apache*. Englewood Cliffs, N.J.: Prentice-Hall, 1974.

MATSON, DANIEL S., and ALBERT H. SCHROEDER. "Cordero's Description of the Apache—1796," *New Mexico Historical Review*, vol. 32, no. 4, 1957.

MERA, HARRY P. *Indian Silverwork of the Southwest Illustrated*. Globe, Ariz.: Dale Stuart King, 1960.

MOORHEAD, MAX L. *The Apache Frontier*. Norman: The University of Oklahoma Press, 1968.

NEWCOMB, FRANC JOHNSON. *Hosteen Klah, Navaho Medicine Man and Sand Painter*. Norman: The University of Oklahoma Press, 1964.

————. *Navajo Omens and Taboos*. Santa Fe, N.M.: The Rydal Press, 1940.

NEWCOMB, W. W., JR. *The Indians of Texas*. Austin: The University of Texas Press, 1961.

OPLER, MORRIS E. *An Apache Life Way: The Economic, Social, and*

Religious Institutions of the Chiricahua Indians. Chicago: The University of Chicago Press, 1941.

———. *Apache Odyssey.* New York: Holt, Rinehart and Winston, 1969.

———. *Childhood and Youth in Jicarilla Apache Society.* Los Angeles: The Southwest Museum, 1946.

PERCEVAL, DON, and CLAY LOCKETT. *A Navajo Sketch Book.* Flagstaff, Ariz.: Northland Press, 1962.

SANTEE, ROSS. *Apache Land.* New York: Charles Scribner's Sons, 1947. Reprinted in paperback by the University of Nebraska Press, Lincoln, 1971.

SCHAAFSMA, POLLY. *Early Navaho Rock Paintings and Carvings.* Santa Fe, N.M.: Museum of Navaho Ceremonial Art, 1966.

SONNICHSEN, C. L. *The Mescalero Apaches.* Norman: The University of Oklahoma Press, 1958.

SPICER, EDWARD H. *Cycles of Conquest, The Impact of Spain, Mexico, and the United States on the Indians of the Southwest, 1533–1960.* Tucson: University of Arizona Press, 1962.

THRAPP, DAN L. *The Conquest of Apacheria.* Norman: The University of Oklahoma Press, 1967.

———. *Victorio and the Mimbres Apaches.* Norman: The University of Oklahoma Press, 1974.

UNDERHILL, RUTH. *Here Come the Navaho.* Lawrence, Kan.: United States Indian Service, 1953.

———. *The Navajos.* Norman: The University of Oklahoma Press, 1956.

WALLACE, ERNEST, and E. ADAMSON HOEBEL. *The Comanches.* Norman: The University of Oklahoma Press, 1952.

WOODWARD, ARTHUR. *A Brief History of Navajo Silversmithing.* Flagstaff, Ariz.: Northern Arizona Society of Science and Art, 1938.

———. "Sidelights on Fifty Years of Apache Warfare," *The Journal of Arizona History,* vol. 11, no. 3, 1961.

YOUNG, ROBERT W. *The Navajo Yearbook.* Window Rock, Ariz.: Navajo Agency, 1961.

Index

217

Howard, General Otis, 72
hunting, 12, 104–106, 125, 140, 142, 184

Indian agents, 56–59, 67, 74, 79, 184
Indian Reorganization Act, 190

Jeffords, Tom, 72
Jicarillas:
  customs of, 108, 110, 117–20, 126, 130–33, 158–59, 172
  history of, 15–16, 32–34, 45, 49, 52, 56, 70, 96
  modern-day, 182, 185, 190, 193, 196, 201
Johnson, James, 50–51
jojoba oil, 195
Jose, Juan, 50–51
Juh, 35, 72, 77–79, 84–86

Kearny, General, 61
Keresan, 9
kinship, 138, 206
  and matrilineal tracing of descent, 44, 138, 206
Kiowa-Apaches, 15–16, 26, 32–34, 46, 52, 95, 108, 110, 120, 126, 130–33, 182
Kiowas, 12, 46
Kirker, James, 51
kivas, 9

languages, 4, 9–11, 15–16, 206
  for warpath, 174
Lawton, Captain H. W., 89
Lincoln, Anthony, 193
linguistics. *See* languages
Lipans:
  customs of, 108, 110, 120, 125–28, 130–33
  history of, 15–16, 26, 30–32, 45–46, 49, 52, 93–94, 95
  modern-day, 182, 191
liquor, 74, 86, 88, 205

livestock, raising of, 26, 30, 43–44, 184–86, 194, 205
Llaneros, 46
local group, 146–48
Loco, 35, 79, 82, 84–87, 93
"Long Walk," the, 64
love magic, 172
Lozen, 141
lumber, 197

McDowell, Camp, 72
magic, 174
  See also witchcraft
Mangas Coloradas, 35, 51, 59–61, 66, 76, 82–84, 87, 91
mano, 118–20
Maricopa tribe, 8, 11
Marion, Fort, 92
marriage, 143–46, 206–207
matrilocal residence, 138–39, 143
medicine men, 154–59, 170–72, 207–209
men, role of, 100–104, 107, 124–25, 159
Mescaleros:
  customs of, 108, 110, 117–18, 120, 126, 130–33, 154–55, 168–69, 171–72
  history of, 15–16, 30–32, 46, 49, 52–53, 59, 63–64, 70, 72, 77, 93, 95, 102–104
  modern-day, 182, 185, 190–91, 193, 196, 200, 202–203
mescal plant, 100–101
metate, 118–20
Mexicans, 16, 22, 35–37, 46–47, 49–50, 52–56, 63, 66, 68, 79, 82, 93, 174, 178, 180, 186–90, 198, 207
Miles, General Nelson A., 88–91
Mimbres, 53, 70, 72, 74, 93, 95, 191
Mogollon Apaches, 53, 70, 72, 74, 93, 95
Mohave tribe, 8, 11, 72
mother-in-law avoidance, 138, 145, 188, 206
Mount Vernon Barracks, 92
mythology, 153, 157